The Wonderful World of Indian Cookery

ROHINI SINGH

PELICAN PUBLISHING COMPANY
Gretna 1994

Published by arrangement with UBS Publishers' Distributors Ltd. (New Delhi)
by Pelican Publishing Company, Inc., 1994

The word "Pelican" and the depiction of a pelican are
trademarks of Pelican Publishing Company, Inc., and are
registered in the U.S. Patent and Trademark Office.

ISBN 1-56554-056-5

Photographs

Maurya Sheraton, New Delhi
India Tourism Development Corporation
Shyam and Anamika Bhargava
C. Shekhar Ahuja, Varsha Tambe, Pramila Parmar
Dhirender Kumar, Ashim Ghosh
P. S. Rao, Pradeep Das Gupta—Fotomedia

Illustrations

Kavita M. Ghildiyal

Printed in Singapore

Published by Pelican Publishing Company, Inc.
1101 Monroe Street, Gretna, Louisiana 70053

This book, featuring
some of 'the bests' of
Indian cuisine, is dedicated
to Kamla and R.P.,
the best of parents — tender,
well-seasoned, with just the
right amount of chilli.

ACKNOWLEDGEMENTS

I turned to many people for help while researching this book. My mother, Kamla Singh, contributed many recipes and shared many culinary secrets with me. Some of her specialities — *Methi Machchi,* Bitter Gourds with Bengal Gram, *Lauki Kofle,* Sindhi Spinach, are included here. My father, an expert cook in his own right, gave me detailed recipes for three of his acknowledged specialities — the *Yakhni Pullao, Kulfi and Paan*. Zarina Chida, a dear friend at whose house we have enjoyed numerous sumptuous *Eid* meals, sat down and painstakingly wrote out the recipes for some special preparations traditionally served on this festive day. I am glad to have the recipes, not only for inclusion in this book but because I like the thought of enjoying *Shikampuri Kabab, Bagara Baingan* and the two vermicelli desserts without having to wait for *Eid. Badi* Aunty (Hardarshan Sandhu) to whom I turn for all kinds of help, culinary and otherwise, not only gave me the recipes for the very special Spicy Chickpeas and *Besan Barfi,* but invited me over to see them being made. Usha Chengappa did the same for the *idli.*

Preet Badhwar, a friend who went away to Indonesia, where she and her family ached for Indian foods, helped me polish up my recipe for *Rasgullas*. From Surinder J. Singh of Jeolikote, I got two delicious recipes typical of the area where she lives — the *Sabut Masur Dal* and Curds flavoured with Mustard. At the *Bukhara,* acknowledged as one of the finest restaurants for *tandoori* food in India, I tasted two mouth-watering delicacies — the *Murgh Malai Kabab* and *Tandoori Pomfret*. They were kind enough to give me the recipes for inclusion in this book. Nirupam Chatterjee contributed some of the Bengali flavours included in this collection — the *Poshto, Ambal* and Mustard Fish. I am grateful to Eera for getting me the recipe for the coconut chutney, to Premila Bhagat for the superb recipe for *Pasanday* and to Anand Singh for demonstrating the very professional *Naans* that are his forté.

All these contributions have immeasurably enriched this collection as have the superb illustrations, painstakingly done by Satish Sud and his office. This book would not have been the same without them.

Contents

1

NOTE

All measurements in cups refer to a cup that holds 8 ounces.

All measurements in spoons are level, unless mentioned otherwise.

All weights are in grams (gms). For conversion to pounds (lbs), you might like to know that

250 gms	=	½ lb
500 gms	=	1 lb
1 kg	=	2 lbs

All vegetables are referred to by names commonly used in India. However, along with their Hindi equivalents, other names by which they are known are also mentioned wherever there is reason for doubt.

In almost all recipes, amounts of salt and chilli to be used are left to the individual cook's discretion to enable each to turn out dishes most suitable for individual preferences.

INTRODUCTION

Welcome to the wide and varied world of Indian cookery, to a sampling of flavours at once diverse and distinctive; a discovery of spices and herbs that enhance and enliven; a combination of foods that surprise and delight.

Our cuisine truly offers a mind-boggling variety of foods and flavours. Influences from the past — Mughal, Persian, Zoroastrian, Portugese— reach out to touch us today through the foods we eat just as local climates, ingredients and needs gently mould them into distinctive specialities of a particular area. The north-west frontier region, for example, contributes the immensely popular method of cooking food in a very special clay oven, the *tandoor,* in which marinated meats, vegetables and even breads cook to unbeatable perfection.

Most of north India, including Punjab, Haryana, Kashmir, Uttar Pradesh and Delhi to this day delight in the legacy of a rich cuisine bequeathed to them by the connoisseurs of food, the Mughals. In addition, each area has also evolved its very own styles. The *Kabab* and *Pasanda,* special cuts of boneless meat, for which Lucknow in Uttar Pradesh is famous jostle for distinction with the special vegetarian food of the state, favoured by the Marwaris, who have settled here. The *pooris,* special deep fried breads, of the area are justifiably famous. The people of Rajasthan, the desert state, make up for the lack of colour in their landscape by flaunting vivid colours in their dress. The bright contrasts seem to extend to the food too — there is plenty of red chilli, and yellow turmeric, in most of the dishes of the area. There is an earthy, robust taste and look to the foods here, just as there is an inherent delicacy to all things Kashmiri, be it the local embroidery, wood-carving or cuisine.

Saffron and other dry fruits, which grow abundantly here, lend it colour and distinction. Cinnamon, mace, nutmeg, cardamom and black pepper 'heat' it, all the better to ward off the long winter chills. *Ver,* a special blend of spices, typifies the cuisine. In contrast, in the naturally warm southern climates, tamarind, coconut and curds take over to impart a cooling influence to the food while fragrant curry leaves and mustard seeds provide a peppy counterpoint. The food is generally light, easily digestible and by being chilli-hot, induces perspiration which is what is needed in the hot climate. In some areas, even the tea is popularly laced with black pepper. The warm weather ferments batters for *idli* (steamed rice cakes) and *dosas* to perfection minus any leavening agents while the sea-coasts add protein-rich seafood to the diet.

Talking of sea-food brings us to another region where its cooking has been perfected — Bengal. The Bay offers a rich haul of fresh fish and shellfish. Rice flourishes in the hot and humid climate as does mustard. Its oil is a

favourite cooking medium in this part of the country. The Bengali boast that no one cook, or savour, fish like a Bengali can, is not totally unfounded. He can talk about food for hours too, quite convinced that there could be no oil more flavourful than mustard, no blend of spices as complete as *Panchphoran* and certainly no sweets as good as the local. And there certainly is an irresistible range to choose from. I think of Bengalis as selective eaters just as I think of Punjabis as hearty, fond-of-good-food ones.

Punjabis will sit down to a meal with an almost infectious relish. And they will eat well, seemingly unmindful of calories — be it a Butter Chicken, a tempting red and floating in *ghee* (clarified butter), *Makhani Dal* (a rich combination of pulses), or if it is winter, a wholesome meal of *Sarson ka Saag* (Mustard Greens) with plenty of *Makki Ki Rotis* (bread made of cornmeal), topped with generous dollops of butter. At home in Punjab, basically an agricultural state, they are quite used to eating meals cooked completely in *ghee*, and washed down by glassfuls of fresh *lassi* (a drink made with curds). A Punjabi who visits Gujarat might come back complaining that everything there tastes sweetish. I prefer to call it a delicious blend of the sweet and salty flavours. Indeed, Gujaratis add a dash of sugar to whatever they may be cooking — a *dal*, a vegetable, a *chivda*, (a spicy snack), *dhokla*, (a kind of steamed cake made of chick-pea flour) — with amazing finesse.

This, however is not the only cuisine in which flavours mingle so judiciously. The Parsis too have blended past and present to produce some palate-tickling preparations. Maharashtra, the state in which many of them have settled, is another region where fish, specially the delectable pomfret, comes into its own. So does rice, which is eaten much more than in the north. This is the state where the sweet, the sour and fiery flavours blend perfectly. If you are sampling a meal at Kolhapur, your tongue would tingle with the heat of it for days! You could, however, hope for the King of Mangoes, the Alphonso to soothe you. But if you still haven't had your fill of hot, spicy food you could move on to Goa, where you can look forward to more sea food and other fiery specialities flavoured with coconut and the locally grown cashews. If you're deciding to cook Goan food, keep a bottle of vinegar handy. It creeps into many preparations, giving them a distinctive flavour.

Still talking of exquisite blending, one comes to Hyderabadi cuisine where again Muslim and south Indian influences blend so very harmoniously — in the exotic, aromatic *Bagara Baingan* (a brinjal speciality), in the *Shikampuri Kabab,* the fragrant *pullaos* and desserts.

But as I rave enthusiastically over the awesome variety of Indian food, let me reassure you in the same breath that there is nothing overcomplicated or unmanageable about cooking an Indian meal. What is essential is a thorough knowledge of herbs and spices, their unique flavourings and combinations. Some basic experimentation will show you just how different each is and also which "goes best" with what.

If you are not already familiar with these varied spices, let me introduce you to them. First, meet the cumins, *(zeera)* — the white one and its darker, tinier, reddish brown, more expensive cousin, *shahzeera*. The second one grows in Kashmir and you will find it flavouring many preparations of the area. Use it if you have it, specially to add a very special touch to *pullaos* or meats. The more common cousin is a great favourite in the north, specially Punjab, U.P. and even Rajasthan. You will encounter it in recipes for *dals,* vegetables, ground in meats, and even sprinkled over a bowl of chilled, beaten curds. It is indeed versatile though it does

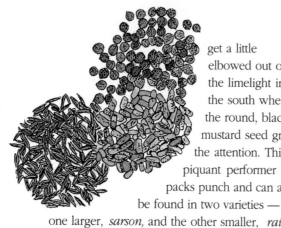

get a little elbowed out of the limelight in the south where the round, black mustard seed grabs the attention. This piquant performer packs punch and can also be found in two varieties — one larger, *sarson,* and the other smaller, *rai.* The first step in many south Indian specialities is spluttering it along with the flattish, brown fenugreek, *methi,* with its deliciously bitter flavouring. Of course, it can be ground and used too — it makes an unusually exciting combination with curds — and certainly, both the seed and its oil are much in demand when you're in the mood for pickling and preserving. Then there is the round, brown coriander seed, *dhaniya.* Though sometimes used whole, it is more often roasted and ground. With a personality all its own, I would however be careful not to let it overpower other flavourings. Used with restraint, it certainly adds to many dishes, specially meats, but get carried away and you might end up with a dark, unappetising result.

After the slightly dominating coriander, you might like to meet the comparatively mild-mannered aniseed, *saunf.* Another seed available in a thinner and fatter variety and looking very much like the cumins, it has an unsubstitutably delicate flavour, whether you use it to lace your tea or flavour a meat or vegetable preparation. A little more persuasive is thymol, *ajwain,* with its pungent, somewhat bitter flavour. You will love it mixed into the dough for your *parathas* (a layered bread), teamed with vegetables too and certainly you will recognise it in some pickles, particularly one made with lemons.

I must also acquaint you now with one of my favourites, the onion seed, *kalonji.* Very popular with Bengali cooks, you will not regret experimenting with this little, black, tear-drop shaped seed. You will see it sitting atop your *Naan,* you can depend on it when you want an unusual tempering for the vegetable you're cooking, particularly brinjals with which it teams exceptionally well and I must tell you that even fish enjoys a sprinkling of this spice. For that matter, there's a sweet mango chutney I make which I can't imagine without it. Another tiny little seed, white this time, is the delicately flavoured sesame, *til.* Extensively used in south Indian cooking, you can make a delicious chutney out of it, use it in a number of desserts or as a delightful tempering for vegetables. You will be pleasantly surprised if you try it with potatoes, for example.

As unprepossessing as the sesame seed is petite, is asafoetida, *hing.* Don't underestimate this stony lump, though. Pound just a pinch and your kitchen will be flooded with a strong, heady aroma. Essential in *dals* of the south, in certain meats and pickles, this resin is certainly worth experimenting with.

And what about when you feel like eating something sour? Take your pick. You could opt for *amchur,* dried mango powder, sprinkled over a cooked vegetable, in stuffing for a *paratha,* or even over a *dal.* Alternately, for a different texture, you could choose pomegranate seeds, *anardana,* which when roasted and ground will not only impart a sour flavour but a tempting blackish colour to your dish. Can you imagine spicy chick-peas without it? Be careful to roast and grind them thoroughly though otherwise you might get complaints that they can be "felt under the teeth." A safer bet, perhaps, in that case is tamarind. Piquantly sour too, it needs some initial treatment before it is used. Leave it to soak in a little water and then, when it softens up, discard the seeds and fibres and sieve out the water and pulp. Add it to *dals*, vegetables, perhaps to meat or chicken, use it in pickles or in fact, make it itself into a delicious, rich brown, sweet-sour chutney, that makes a perfect finishing touch served over curds with dumplings, *dahi pakori,* for example.

When you're in the mood for some specially exotic cooking, you could enlist the help of poppy seeds, *khas khas,* a small, round, ivory coloured seed that's an excellent thickener and also has a special, almost nutty flavour. When you are in the mood for special cooking, in fact, you will appreciate having saffron, *kesar,* in your cupboard. Just a few strands soaked in a little milk or water and stirred in to meats, rice or desserts, will reward you with an unbeatably delicate golden colour and an appetising aroma and flavour.

Talking of golden colourings, you must be familiar with turmeric, *haldi,* a member of the ginger family. It's most likely that you've met it as a yellow powder, responsible for the colour of your *dal* and many vegetables. Of course, *dals* particularly, would look and taste pale and listless without a dash of this but I wouldn't overdo it. As with most other spices, judicious use of it is best. Overly coloured vegetables are a bad habit and too much turmeric often swamps natural colours and even flavours.

Have I left out anything? I just haven't come to the whole spices yet, each of them more aromatic and special than the next — the sweetish, woody cinnamon, *dalchini,* spicy cloves, *laung,* the cardamoms, *elaichi,* one black and more dominating, the other green and more delicate, nutmeg, *jaiphal,* and mace without which you cannot imagine Indian cooking. Responsible for the appetising aromas of rice, essential in most meat preparations, used in some *dals* and for a touch of the unusual in vegetables, your spice-shelf would certainly seem incomplete without them. Best roasted and ground freshly before being used, you just cannot hope to substitute them with the commercially available brands. To maximise and release their aromas and flavours, drop the whole spices into hot oil, and let them splutter for a few minutes before you start the cooking process. Alternately, sprinkle over some of the ground *masala* to finish the dish.

By the way, there is yet another dimension to these spices. In addition to their other virtues, they have almost medicinal values too. That tiny pinch of asafoetida, for example, aids digestion and so you will often find it in preparations that might otherwise be considered hard to digest. Thymol too and for that matter, aniseed and mint are carminative. Complaints of heaviness and upset stomachs are often simply cured by grinding thymol and swallowing it with water. And there's certainly nothing better after a heavy Indian meal than chewing on some cardamom to help the food go down. Cloves too, for that matter, are an antidote to indigestion and are efficacious for many aches and pains. If your appetite seems to be sluggish, nutmeg or nigella might help. Need a laxative? The most natural one is basil.

What might be interesting for you to know is that there are "warm spices" which generate heat in the body and "cool spices" which naturally, do the opposite. Logically, the weather dictates the ones you should be using to feel most comfortable. As I mentioned earlier, the warm spices, for example, cinnamon, mace, nutmeg, black cardamom and black pepper "heat" Kashmiri cuisine while the cool spices — green cardamom, cloves, aniseed — will be found in recipes popular in summer, or in your after-dinner, digestive *paan.* That gives you just some idea of the intricacies of Indian recipes, often providing antidotes without your even knowing it!

There is just one more fascinating aspect that I would like to mention. You can manipulate somewhat the character of most of these spices depending on when during the cooking process you add them. Cumin, for example, imparts a different flavour and look if the whole seed is dropped into hot oil. It gains in colour and aroma if it is roasted and ground and then added to a dish and certainly, if you begin by allowing it to get too dark, you have started on the wrong foot! Similarly, you can experiment with mustard seed. I am sure you can imagine the different results you can expect. This applies to most of these spices and I am sure you will enjoy discovering and making the most of these subtle nuances in their characters.

The secret of cooking well lies, in fact, in capitalising on these spices and of course complimenting them with some herbs — the mild-mannered dill, *soya*, utterly refreshing coriander, (cilantro) fragrantly spicy curry leaves, *kari patta*, aromatic bay leaves, *tez patta*, cooling mint, *pudina* and the sharp, sweetish-bitter basil, *tulsi*. Each has its own preferences. Dill flavours Split Gram, *mung dal*, beautifully as it does too chicken or a delicate cucumber *raita* or salad. Curry leaves perk up whatever they are added to, be it a meat, *dal*, or a vegetable. Of course, I can't imagine *sambhar*, a south Indian speciality without them just as I couldn't have imagined an omellete enlivened by their addition. I must admit they're both delicious! Mint harmonises excellently with potatoes, curds or even rice and as for fresh coriander, I am addicted to it. Not only does it add a delightfully fresh flavour, it also gives your dish a refreshing green counter-point. I add it usually almost at the end of the cooking time so that it loses neither value.

A discovery of these little tips and tricks is the secret of Indian cooking. To become a distinctive cook, you must, in fact, learn to not only use these spices and herbs in happy conjunction with each other, you must practise highlighting just one or other of them. Nervous beginners tend to throw in all or at the least, too many, hoping for a good result. What actually happens is that all flavours get smothered indistinguishably. An experienced cook, on the other hand, allows just that particular herb or spice to come into its own. Just cumin to flavour potatoes for example, the overriding flavour of cardamom in a chicken dish, fennel flavouring meat or fish spiced with mustard seed. The combinations are endless. And personally inspired.

That is the other wonder of our cuisine. It allows for unlimited creativity. Just as a good gardener is said to have green fingers, so it is often said that a good cook has a particular expertise "in his or her hand." That could well be another way of saying that he or she has honed the art of blending spices and herbs to an almost instinctive perfection. Develop it, master it and you too will delight in the secret of "good cooking in your hand."

Before I end, I must make one confession. One of the most difficult parts of writing this book was selecting the recipes for inclusion in this collection, from amongst the large number I had collected. If it so happens that you do not find in these pages some particular speciality that you're looking for, I hope you will be amply compensated by another that you might happen to try out. I have tried to bring to you the varied flavours of our cuisine and I hope I have succeeded in highlighting some of the more unusual ones.

I would like to say a special word of welcome to those who are unfamiliar with Indian foods and to whom this book will serve as an introduction to our rich cuisine. May your discovery be rewarding. For those who already know and love this cuisine, those to whom this heritage belongs, may this collection be an enriching offering.

And to each of you, happy experimenting and eating!

—R.S.

THE MAGIC
OF GRIDDLE AND
ROLLING PIN

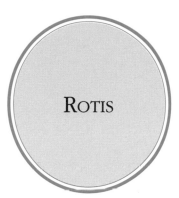

ROTIS

Indian Breads

Flours-wholewheat, refined, a mixture of the two, gramflour (*besan*), and cornmeal (*makki*) are indeed an indispensable part of an Indian menu, used as they are to make one or other kind of *roti*, without which most Indian meals would be quite incomplete. Indian bread—the *chappati, phulka, mani, poli, rotli*—call it what you will, is very much taken for granted on our table. That, however, neither makes it as simple to cook as the recipe sounds nor wholly similar in every part of the country. You cannot just go out and buy it as you do bread, abroad. The dough must be kneaded at home, for each day's requirements, and the *rotis*, made freshly before each meal. I think I could safely state that each cook, in time to come, develops her own method of doing it. The amount of dough she pinches off, how much she flattens it, how much dry flour she uses and when, how often and at exactly which moment in the whole process, she turns it on the *tava* (heavy griddle) all becomes a matter of deep-seated and unalterable habit. To see a perfectly rounded, evenly rolled out *chappati* sit on the fire, wobble slightly as it gets to its feet and then puff up with air, is nothing short of magical. It testifies to the dough being well kneaded, the *chappati* being well rolled out, being put on the *tava* at the right temperature and being turned over at the right moment. It is testimony too, to the deftness of hand and concentration involved—both qualities cooks and magicians need in no small measure.

Read in many books, the recipe for making a *chappati* sounds one of the easiest, to which you barely spare a thought. I have tried to make the one included here as precise as possible, even measuring out the water needed to make the dough. I must admit, however, that this is, at best, an approximation and you will have to use your own judgement as you go along. Perhaps I didn't mention earlier that even the consistency of the dough becomes a matter of preference and so differs from cook to cook. To make things easier, however, I have tried to look at the whole procedure through the eyes of a novice and have pointed out the steps one often takes for granted. Even then, beginners must expect to be patient and preferably put up, before they start, a placard that serves to remind them that practice makes perfect. In the case of *chappati* making, truly, no amount of theorising, watching or advice can make it all happen like practice can.

Before we come to the recipes, a word about the equipment you will need. To knead the dough, a flat-bottomed, largeish plate with

13

shallow sides (it looks somewhat like an over-sized pastry pan) is most convenient. To roll out the *chappati*, you will need a *belna* or rolling pin, as also a *chakla*. This is a marble or wooden board usually about 9 inches in diameter, slightly raised on three squat legs. You can, I am sure, substitute it easily, using even a clean marble counter-top. Finally, you need a *tava*, a heavy, black, concave cast-iron griddle. It could be with or without a handle though the one which has one is usually easier to use, specially if you prefer completing the cooking of your *chappati* on an open fire (see recipe). Additionally, you might need a sieve to ensure that the flour you are using is minus impurities. A small bowl, preferably wide-mouthed, comes in handy to keep by your side the dry flour you will be using during the cooking process.

The first recipe in this section tells you how to go about making an everyday *chappati*. Once you've mastered that, you can go on to trying out a more elaborate *paratha*, a sort of layered *chappati*. It keeps very well and so is an excellent idea for tiffins, office-lunches, picnics and travel. When you're confident enough, you can try stuffing it with all manner of things from eggs to cottage cheese to potato to minced meat. You will find some suggestions here and you can surely think up some more. Apart from *parathas*, you will encounter the popular, specially with children, *poori*, a deep-fried bread, an utterly delicious *besan roti*, a bread made with gram-flour as well as a professional, home-made *naan*, quite different in looks and flavour from the others. This one is fair, made as it is with flour, sourish since the dough is kneaded with curds (yogurt) and then fermented and when cooked, should be very soft. Normally made in a *tandoor*, a clay oven, the recipe included here shows you how to manage it successfully in your kitchen. Another bread that's kneaded with curds instead of water is the one for the *bhatura*. Instead of being roasted, however, this one is fried and usually served with a chickpea preparation.

If you're already adept at all these varieties, you can move on to the next section but if you're a beginner to Indian cooking, sooner or later, I guess you'll be thumbing through these pages. Before going any further, I must admit that this is a far from comprehensive collection—books have been written on the subject—but I have deliberately included a selection that can be made easily at home without very fancy gadgetry or special equipment.

CHAPPATI

A plain, roasted bread.
This is the everyday, taken for-granted
accompaniment to most menus.

INGREDIENTS
2 cups wheatflour, sieved
³/₄ cup plus a few tablespoons water
Dry Flour

UTENSILS
A shallow plate with a raised edge
A griddle
A rolling pin
A separate bowl to keep the dry flour
A clean cloth (optional)
A marble or wooden board to roll out the
dough

Method

1. Put the flour in the plate. Make a well in the centre and pour in some water. With your fingertips, start mixing it with the flour. Keep adding water as needed. As you go on, you will find the dough getting more manageable and less sticky. Finally, you should have a flexible, but not sticky dough. Your fingers should remain clean even when you handle it. You will now be able to knead it easily. Press down on it with your knuckles, flattening it out as you do so, then fold over and start all over again. If at all you feel the dough is too dry or tends to get cracks in it, dip your fingertips in water, pat the dough with them and continue. Occasionally,

press down with your palms. Keep at it for at least 5 minutes then cover it with a clean cloth and keep aside for at least half an hour and a little longer if possible. If you start making *chappatis* with it immediately, you will find they are brittle and hard.

2. Put the griddle onto the fire.

3. To make the *chappati*, pinch off a piece of dough (if it has been lying in the fridge, knead it a little before starting), a little larger than a medium–sized lemon. Roll it into a ball, making sure there are no cracks in it, and flatten it slightly between the palms. Dip into the dry flour, coat both sides lightly and put it onto the rolling board.

4. Start rolling it out with a rolling pin. One side will automatically get a little elongated. Dust with dry flour and keeping the elongated side horizontally now on the board, roll out so you get a circle. From now on, keep the pressure as light as possible, so that soon enough you will find the *chappati* gradually rotating with the movement of the rolling pin. When you are able to do this, the *chappati* will automatically get evenly rolled out. If you press down too hard on the rolling pin, the *chappati* will remain stationary and you will have a misshapen shape instead of a neat circle. Dust with dry flour whenever you need. Give the edges an extra roll to avoid them getting left thicker and consequently, uncooked.

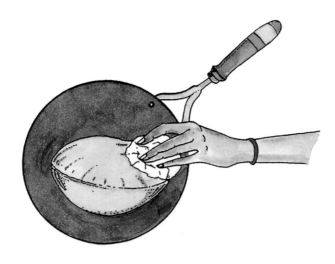

5. To check that the griddle is heated to the right temperature, drop a pinch of dry flour onto it. It should turn reddish golden in a few seconds. Dust it off and slap the rolled out *chappati* on. In under a minute, you will see little bumps start to form on the surface and the underside should have brown flecks all over. It is time to turn it over. When the second side is also similarly cooked, take the *chappati* off the griddle and removing the griddle from the fire, let the *chappati* sit directly on the fire. If you have done everything right, it should puff up. Turn over briefly on the other side, if at all necessary, and serve with a dot of butter or *ghee*.

There is an alternative way of doing this last step. If you don't want to finish the cooking of the *chappati* directly on the fire, let it remain on the griddle, and press down on it, with a clean, folded cloth, at various points. It should still puff up.

Makes approximately 14 chappatis, 5 inches in diameter.

Note: If you need to warm up chappatis *that have been made considerably before the meal, here's a simple method. Wrap them in foil, put a little less than a cup of water in a pressure cooker or steamer, place the wrapped* chappatis *on the trivet on a plate and let them get warmed through by steam. You will not need to put the weight on the cooker. Just cover, let the steam form and take out in a few minutes. You can also try deep–frying them to give them a new lease of life.*

PARATHA

A flaky layered bread.
This is the simplest kind. Perfect it before you
experiment with the more elaborate ones.

INGREDIENTS
2 cups wheatflour, sieved
³/₄ cup plus a few tablespoons water
Oil or ghee *for frying*
Dry flour

UTENSILS
A shallow plate with a raised edge
A griddle
A rolling pin
A marble or wooden board to roll out the dough
A small bowl to keep the dry flour
A small bowl for the oil or ghee
A teaspoon

Method

1. Knead the dough. The method is the same as for making *chappatis*.

2. Put the griddle on to the fire.

3. Pinch off a piece of the dough. It would be larger than what you need to make an ordinary *chappati*. Roll it into a ball. Flatten slightly between the palms. Dust on both sides with the dry flour and lay on the rolling board.

4. Start rolling it with the rolling pin—you should make the circle approximately 4 inches in diameter. Smear about half a teaspoonful of oil or *ghee* over the surface, sprinkle a pinch of dry flour all over and fold the circle in half. You now have a semicircle. Repeat the procedure of smearing with oil and flour and fold again to make a triangle.

5. Dust on both sides with dry flour and roll out as evenly as possible to a little more than double its size.

6. Test the griddle as for the *chappati*. Slap on the *paratha*. As soon as flecks start to form, turn over and cook on the other side. When that too is a little more than half-done, take half a teaspoon of oil and smear it over the surface. Turn this side downwards and smear the same amount of oil on the surface now uppermost. Press down with the spoon on the thicker edges to ensure they get cooked through. Turn over once more before serving.

7. If your *paratha* is not as soft as it should be, you are probably rolling it too thin or over-cooking and allowing a brownish crust to form before you turn it over the first time. So turn it quicker and you should notice the difference.

Makes approximately 10 parathas.

For an interesting difference you can add salt as well as thymol seeds (ajwain) *to the flour before kneading or even some some mango pickle. Dried mint or fenugreek generously sprinkled over before serving also makes for added flavour.*

BHARWAN PARATHA

A stuffed layered bread.
This is the meal-in-itself paratha.
These are best served with chilled curds
and a selection of pickles. Cater for a nap soon after.

INGREDIENTS

2 cups wheatflour, sieved
$^3/_4$ cup plus a few tablespoons water
Oil or ghee for frying
Dry flour

UTENSILS

A shallow plate with a raised edge
A griddle
A rolling pin
A wooden or marble board to roll out the
dough
A separate bowl to keep the dry flour
A small bowl for the oil or ghee
A teaspoon

Method

1. Knead the dough. The method is the same as for making *chappatis*.

2. Put the griddle on to the fire.

3. Pinch off a piece of the dough. It would be larger than what you need for a normal *chappati*. Roll it into a ball, and flatten slightly between the palms. Dust both sides with dry flour and lay it on the rolling board.

4. Start rolling with the rolling pin—make the circle approximately 4 inches in diameter. Pick it off the board and cup it in your left hand. Put a teaspoon or two (you will be able to put more as you get experienced) of stuffing (see note) into the centre of the dough. With your right hand start pulling the edges of the circle closed over the stuffing. Press with your fingertips to seal.

5. Seam side down first, dust on both sides with dry flour. Lay on the board.

6. Gently roll out. Keep the pressure very light and if you find the stuffing oozing out or the dough tearing, sprinkle a little dry flour and keep on till you have a reasonable sized *paratha*.

7. Test the griddle and continue making the *paratha* (from step 6) as you do the unstuffed one.

Makes 10 parathas.

Ideas for stuffings

1. Grate cauliflower. For the amount of dough mentioned, a medium sized one should suffice. Add to it finely chopped fresh coriander, chopped fresh green chillies, and fresh, chopped ginger. Just before making the *parathas*, add salt and coriander powder to taste.

2. Grate radish. Just before cooking, add salt and spices.

3. Grate a combination of radish, carrot and add to it some finely chopped, fresh fenugreek. This *paratha* is jokingly referred to as the 'patriotic *paratha*' since it contains an orange, white and green stuffing!

4. Using onions, fresh coriander, green chillies, make a scrambled egg mixture. You should be able to stuff at least 3 parathas with each egg, presuming that you will use 1 small onion and 1 tomato plus greens with it. Cottage cheese can be scrambled similarly for a change.

5. Cook peas (see the recipe for Peas with Cottage Cheese).

6. Cook minced meat (see section on meats).

7. Dry Bengal gram. For this variation, you can either dry out left-over *dal*, sprinkle a little *garam masala* over, add a little lime juice for added flavour and use it as a stuffing. Alternately, you can cook *Sookha Dal* (see section on pulses).

8. Boil and mash potatoes. 3 large ones should be sufficient to stuff 10 parathas. To the potatoes add fresh, chopped coriander, chopped green chillies, salt and a sprinkle of coriander powder. Those who prefer sour flavours can try adding dry mango powder or crushed pomegranate seeds. A sprinkle of dried fenugreek makes for a refreshing change.

9. Use almost any mashed up, dry left-overs.

BHATURA

A fried bread made with flour and curds.
Slightly sour, white and fluffy, bhaturas *are traditionally eaten*
with chick-peas and potatoes. The dough is kneaded with curds
instead of water and bhaturas *do make for an interesting,*
though heavy, change.

INGREDIENTS

3 cups plain flour, sieved
$^1/_2$ teaspoon baking soda, sieved with the flour
1 teaspoon salt, sieved with the flour
1 $^1/_4$ cup curds, lightly beaten
1 teaspoon sugar, mixed with the curds

UTENSILS

A shallow plate with a raised edge
A griddle
A rolling pin
A wooden or marble board to roll out the
dough
A pan for deep frying
A long-handled, slotted spoon

Method

1. Put the flour in the plate. Knead in the same way as for the *chappatis*, adding the curds a little at a time till you have a firm but not sticky dough. Cover and keep aside—in the winter you should leave it overnight; in the summer, 5-6 hours will do.

2. Heat the oil in the pan. Since you have to deep-fry, you will need at least half a panful.

3. Start to roll out the *bhaturas*. Pinch off a piece of dough— about the same amount as you need for a normal *chappati*. Roll it and flatten slightly by pressing between the palms. Roll out as you do a *poori*—with the help of a few drops of oil on each side. If you don't turn it around, you will automatically roll it elongated, into a kind of tear-drop shape. Drop into the hot oil. It should not be as hot as that needed by *pooris*. Also, it will take a shorter time to fry—the end result is basically white with a few flecks of brown. As it starts to fluff up—and this will happen in a few seconds after you drop it in, turn over and after another few seconds, take out. Drain, if needed, before serving.

Makes approximately 15 bhaturas.

POORI

A light fried bread.
Without knowing the name, a Czech friend
requested me to make these. This is how she described them—
they're brown, very light and filled with air.
So they are and what many of us fantasize
about when we're away from home.

INGREDIENTS
1 cup wheatflour, sieved
1 cup plain flour, sieved
1 cup water
Oil for frying

UTENSILS
A shallow plate with a raised edge
A rolling pin
A wooden or marble board to roll out the dough
A long-handled, flat, slotted spoon
A heavy bottomed pan for frying, preferably a
karhai *or wok.*

Method
1. Mix the two flours and knead as for a
chappati. Set aside for a few hours.
2. Heat the oil. Since you have to deep-fry, you
will need at least half a panful. Let the oil heat
up to just below smoking point.
3. Pinch off a piece of dough. You will need
about the same as you use for a *chappati* and if
you want slightly smaller *pooris*, a little less. Put
a few drops of oil onto the rolling board, lay the
slightly flattened dough on it, put a few more
drops of oil on top and roll out. You do not use

dry flour to dust, hence the oil to keep the
dough from sticking to the rolling-pin or board.
4. As soon as the *poori* is evenly rolled out, drop
into the hot oil. Keep the spoon ready in your
hand. As the *poori* starts rising to the surface, pat
it a couple of times and it will swell up. Turn
over and after a couple of seconds on the other
side, take it out. You can decide whether you
want it just golden brown and softer or crisper.
5. Don't be disappointed if the first *poori* isn't a
great success. They will become better and
better as you learn more about temperature
control.

Makes approximately 12-15 pooris.

Note: You may also use milk instead of water
to knead the dough for melt-in-the-mouth
pooris.

To make luchchis, *which are quite similar,*
use only plain flour for the dough to which a
little fat is added before kneading. You may
also salt them. The water needed will naturally
be a little less because of the added fat content.
For 2 cups flour, you should need about 2
tablespoons of fat, normally ghee.

METHI ROTI

A fenugreek flavoured bread.
A delightful roti *that you can enjoy, however, only when*
fresh fenugreek (methi) *is in season. Here are two ways of*
making it. Try both and decide which you prefer.

INGREDIENTS
250 grams fresh fenugreek,
picked and washed
1-2 green chillies
2-3 cloves garlic
A small piece of ginger
(optional)
Salt to taste
1 ½ cups wheatflour
Oil for frying

UTENSILS
A shallow plate with a raised edge
A rolling pin
A griddle
A marble or wooden board to roll out
the dough
A small bowl to keep the dry flour
A small bowl for the oil or ghee
A teaspoon

Method
1. Grind the fenugreek with all the ingredients
except the flour. Use only about cup of water.
2. Knead the dough with the ground paste.
You should get about 1 cup. Add as
much flour as you need to make a soft but not
sticky dough.
3. Make the *roti* as you would a normal *paratha*.

Makes approximately 10 rotis.

Note: The alternative way of doing this, which
is also very popular, is: wash, pick and finely
chop the fenugreek as well as the chillies. You
can also add 1 medium onion, finely chopped.
You may or may not add the garlic and
ginger. Add the salt. Put all these ingredients
into the dry flour and knead as you would
normal chappati *dough, with water.*

BESAN ROTI

*A bread made
with gramflour.
Though heavy, this ranks as
one of my favourite
changes.*

INGREDIENTS

1 cup wheatflour

1 cup gramflour

¹/₂ –1 cup water

2 small onions, finely chopped

1–2 green chillies, finely chopped

Salt to taste

Oil for frying

UTENSILS

A shallow plate with a raised edge

A griddle

A rolling pin

*A wooden or marble board to roll out the
dough*

A bowl to keep the dry flour

A small bowl for the oil or ghee

A teaspoon

Method

1. Put all the dry ingredients in the plate. Knead
as you would for a *paratha*, with the
water. Keep aside for at least half
an hour.

2. Roll out like a chappati.
Fry as you would an
ordinary *paratha*.

3. These *rotis* are best
enjoyed with curds or as
a change for breakfast with
a pickle.

Makes approximately 10 rotis.

*Note: A few teaspoons of oil or ghee added to the
dry ingredients before kneading the dough makes
for a softer roti.*

NAAN

A bread made with flour and curds.
Soft, white, deliciously different from the everyday
roti. *Here's a recipe that, with a little practice, will give you really*
professional results. These naans *go best with*
black gram dal *and a meat.*

INGREDIENTS

4 cups plain flour
2-2 $\frac{1}{2}$ cups curds, lightly beaten
3 tablespoons oil
1 teaspoon sugar
$\frac{1}{2}$ teaspoon salt
2 eggs, lightly beaten (optional)
A pinch of baking powder
Sesame or onion seeds (til or kalonji)

UTENSILS

A shallow plate with a raised edge
Two clean cloths
A rolling pin
An old pressure cooker without an inward-curving rim or a heavy pan with a handle and straight sides
Oven gloves

Method

1. Knead all the ingredients together except the seeds. Do this at least 3 hours in advance of cooking the *naans*. Keep the dough aside, covered with a clean cloth.
2. Before you want to make the *naans*, put the pan or cooker on to the fire to heat it thoroughly.

3. Roll the *naans*—each should be about the size of your palm. Traditionally, they are tear-drop shaped—you can stretch one side a little. If you find the dough is sticking, use a few drops of oil to help roll it out. Sprinkle a few sesame or onion seeds over. You can do at least six at a time.

Wear an oven glove. Roll a clean cloth into a ball. Stretch another cloth smoothly over it. Take a *naan*, put it onto the rolled up cloth and slap it onto the side of the cooker. Just in case it doesn't stick, wet it with a little water on one side and press it on. You should be able to stick on at least 5. Do it quickly, so the pan doesn't cool down.
4. After about 4-5 minutes, turn the pan over so the inside is directly over the flame. Keep another few minutes, then, take off one and see if the side that was stuck on is cooked. If needed, put the other side on to the fire for a few seconds before you serve it.

Makes 12-15 naans.

THEPLA

*An ingenious Gujarati combination of rice and wheatflour.
It's a good idea to use up leftover rice too in
a totally unrecognisable form.*

INGREDIENTS

1 cup boiled rice
1 cup wheatflour, sieved
1-2 green chillies, finely chopped
*2 teaspoons sesame seeds (*til*)*
Salt to taste
A pinch of turmeric powder
¼ – ½ cup curds, lightly beaten
Oil for frying

UTENSILS

A shallow plate with a raised edge
A griddle
*A marble or wooden board to roll out the
dough*
A small bowl to keep the dry flour
A rolling pin
A small bowl for the oil or ghee
A teaspoon

Method

1. Lightly mash the rice.

2. Into the wheat flour, mix all the dry ingredients—the chillies, seeds, salt and turmeric.

3. Mix the rice and wheat together. Knead into a soft but not sticky dough with the curds. Use only as much as you need. Keep the dough aside for at least half an hour, covered with a clean cloth.

4. Put the griddle on to heat. Make as you would a *paratha*. Serve immediately.

Makes approximately 12 theplas.

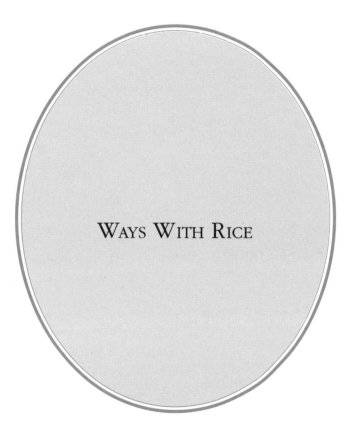

WAYS WITH RICE

CHAWAL

Rice

Rice, like the *rotis* in the last section, is an indispensable part of an Indian menu. Many communities in our country, particularly in the south, could hardly imagine life without it. Served boiled, with *dal* (pulses), curds and relishes, it makes a balanced and popular meal. More distinctive in *pullaos*—the fragrant pea, the delicate Goan, the spicy Sindhi, the Kashmiri *Yakhni*—garnished with nuts and a tempting sprinkle of crunchy, fried onions, it is very much party fare. But these are only two of it's incarnations. You may not recognize it but it's there in your *dosa*; the Gujarati *thepla*, and for that matter, it features in a number of traditional Indian sweets. Talking of its many uses, I even drop a teaspoon of uncooked rice into my tempering of *sambhar dal* (see section on Pulses). It imparts an unusual, nutty flavour.

I don't want to sound discouraging again, but like the everyday *chappati*, perfect everyday boiled rice is as common as commonsense. Cooked just right—not too mushy, yet not undercooked, with each grain separate and unbroken, a steaming just-turned-out-plateful is a delight. And again, it's one of those things that every cook has her own recipe for. One will cook in a large quantity of water, which is then drained away; another wouldn't dream of doing that, since she feels it loses much of its nutritional value; one will measure the water to the cupful while her neighbour will pour it to "one-finger-level" above the rice in the pan and swear that that is indeed the only accurate method. The first recipe in this section tells you how I go about it. You might just like to try it out, even if it's not *your* preferred method!

Generally, all rice needs to be picked to get rid of the occasional husk and other impurities that may be lurking in it. Then it should be washed in a number of changes of water—in fact, till the water runs clear—and then left to soak before cooking. Older, maturer rice can take a longer soaking; younger rice can't be left too long or you risk it breaking up during cooking. To cook, I always measure out the water. Again, older rice cooks best in exactly double the quantity of water; younger rice needs a little less to be cooked to perfection. The method I generally like to follow is to first cook the rice on high heat till most of the water evaporates. Then, I reduce the heat, put a griddle under the pan and put the rice on *dum*. This is the last stage of cooking, during which the rice tenderises fully, the water evaporates

and in fact, the cooking process is completed by steam on a very slow fire. This is a particularly important stage when you are cooking *pullaos*, because it's the time when the flavours of the rice and whatever it is being cooked with, be it meat or peas or fenugreek, mingle with each other as the rice cooks slowly to perfection. It is a good idea to use a pan with a tight fitting cover which can be weighted down (with a mortar) to ensure the flavours are all sealed in. This can also be done with a dough made of wheatflour and water which is pressed round the lid.

Of course, recipes and methods apart, there is no over-emphasizing the fact that good quality, old, mature rice naturally makes for better results.

Talking about mature rice, it's a good idea to buy as much as you can conveniently store, and hoard it for at least two years before you use it. To keep rice weevils at bay, wash and dry *neem* leaves, which have antiseptic properties, and sprinkle them in the canister. Alternately, lightly coat the rice with turmeric powder. This can be washed off when you use the rice and even if the rice still retains a pale yellowish tinge, it will make no difference to the taste. Another tip that I picked up during my travels in Coorg, the home of pepper, is to put a layer of whole pepper-corns at the bottom of the canister along with sprinkling some among the rice. I have tried this method and can vouch that it is very effective. Again, you can remove the pepper-corns if you don't wish to use them in the particular recipe you're trying out. You can also buy commercially sold mercury tablets, which

again have to mixed in with the rice when you store it. Of course, you have to be *very* careful to remove them before you cook.

Apart from plain rice, there are some tempting *pullaos* in this section. As you will notice, there are two meat-based ones. I have deliberately chosen them because they illustrate two different methods of preparation. In one, the meat is cooked separately and is then layered with the rice and the whole mixture is put on *dum.* In the *Yakhni,* on the other hand, the meat is boiled with spices and the rice is then cooked in the same stock. The second version is slightly lighter and this recipe is particularly vigilant as far as the quantity of oil used is concerned. Those who normally shy away from trying a meat-*pullao* because it's too heavy, can indulge themselves with this one, with no harmful after-effects. There is a mild coconut flavoured rice for a light change and a more dominating fenugreek flavoured one. The section could hardly be complete without the famous lemon-rice and *dahi-chawal* (rice with curds) from the south. There is a recipe for rice flavoured with corn and capsicum that came about quite by chance when corn and capsicums were in season, and that is now an established family favourite.

The variety I have selected for you in this section will not only illustrate that the rice on your table must have ambitions far beyond being just an accompaniment but that it can be a much talked about and complimented preparation. I hope that it will inspire you to invent more new and interesting recipes with this staple of our diet.

UBLE CHAWAL

Boiled Rice.
This is the traditional recipe that uses
double the measure of water for the rice,
and follows the method whereby the rice is first cooked on high heat
and much of the water evaporated, after which it is left on
a slow fire to complete the cooking process.

INGREDIENTS
2 cups rice, picked and washed in a number
of changes of water
4 cups water
Salt to taste (optional)

UTENSILS
A heavy-bottomed pan with
a tight fitting lid
A griddle

Method
1. Soak the rice in the measured water for at least half an hour.
2. Put on the fire with the salt. Cook, covered, on high heat till the water reaches the level of the rice, than reduce heat, put the griddle underneath the pan, cover it tightly and cook for about 15 minutes. Open the pan, check that the water has all evaporated (you will see holes in the surface of the rice) and that the rice has cooked completely. Fluff up lightly with the back of a spoon and if possible, serve immediately.

Serves 4.

Note: To reheat leftover rice, put it into a lidded pan. Put the pan into a pressure cooker or large pan into which about a cup of water has been poured. Put the lid on, without the weight. Put it on the fire. As soon as the water starts boiling and the steam forms, it will heat the rice through, almost as good as new. It should not take more than a few minutes.

CHHOLIYA PULLAO

*Rice with Green Chick-peas.
One of my favourite
combinations that you can
unfortunately enjoy only
when green chick-peas are
in season.*

INGREDIENTS

*3 tablespoons cooking oil
1 large black cardamom, pounded
1 teaspoon cumin seeds
3 large onions, sliced in semi-circles
1¹/₂ - 2" piece ginger, sliced finely or chopped
3-4 cloves garlic, crushed (optional)
250 grams green chick-peas, washed
2 stock cubes, vegetarian or non-vegetarian
2 cups rice, picked, washed and soaked in 4
cups water
Salt to taste*

UTENSILS

*A large heavy-bottomed pan with a
tight-fitting lid
A griddle
A weight*

Method

1. Heat the oil. Drop in the cardamom.
2. After a few seconds, add the cumin seeds and in another few seconds, the sliced onions. Fry light brown.
3. Add the ginger and if you're using it, the garlic. Fry another few minutes.
4. Add the chick-peas and fry till they turn light brownish.
5. Add the stock cubes, the rice with the water in which it has been soaking, and the salt. Raise the heat and let the liquid start boiling and reach the level of the rice, then lower the heat, put the griddle underneath the pan, the weight on top and cook another 20-25 minutes.
6. Open the pan, check that the rice is done and that all the water has evaporated. Fluff gently with the back of a spoon and if you're not ready to serve, keep it tightly covered on the hot griddle (though off the fire).

Serves 4-6.

Note: For green chick-peas, you may substitute parboiled, dry ones or fresh peas. The pea pullao is very popular and very satisfying. I personally don't like even a dal with it though plain curds or a raita are very complimentary.

METHI CHAWAL

Fenugreek Rice.
An interesting blend of flavours that I first tasted at
a Maharashtrian friend's house. Though undoubtedly more flavourful
with fresh fenugreek, you may try it with the dried too,
it you feel inclined.

INGREDIENTS
250 grams fresh, washed and chopped, or 5-6
teaspoons dried fenugreek
3 tablespoons cooking oil
1" piece cinnamon
3-4 cloves
1 black cardamom
½-1 teaspoon whole
black peppercorns
2 onions,
chopped fine
1" piece of
ginger, ground
3-4 cloves garlic,
ground
½ teaspoon turmeric
powder
2 green chillies
(optional), chopped
Salt to taste
2 cups rice, picked, washed and
soaked in 4 cups water

UTENSILS
A heavy-bottomed pan with a tight-fitting lid
A griddle
A weight

Method

1. Boil the fresh fenugreek in water for about 10 minutes. Drain, grind and keep aside.

2. Heat the oil and add the next four ingredients.

3. After a minute or so, add the onions and fry till pinkish.

4. Add the ginger and garlic pastes and fry till golden brown.

5. Add the turmeric, chillies and salt and fry a few seconds.

6. Add the ground or dry fenugreek and saute for a few minutes.

7. Add the rice and fry along with the rest of the ingredients. When it starts sticking to the bottom of the pan, add the water in which the rice was soaked. Turn the heat to high. After the liquid starts boiling and reaches the level of the rice, reduce heat, cover the pan tightly, put the weight on top, slide the griddle underneath and cook about 25 minutes.

8. Open the pan, check that the rice is done and all the liquid has evaporated. Fluff up gently with the back of a spoon before serving.

Serves 4.

BHUTTE-MIRCH WALE CHAWAL

Rice cooked with Corn and Capsicum.
Make this as often as you can when
both vegetables are at their freshest best—
it is such an aromatic and unusual
blending of flavours.

INGREDIENTS
2 large ears of corn
3 tablespoons cooking oil
1 black cardamom, pounded
1 teaspoon cumin seeds
3 onions, sliced
1 ½ piece of ginger, ground
1 large capsicum, (bell-pepper) ribbed and chopped
Salt, pepper and chilli to taste
2 cups rice, picked, washed and soaked

UTENSILS
A pressure cooker
A heavy-bottomed pan with a tight-fitting lid
A griddle
A weight

Method

1. Boil the corn in about 4 cups of water till tender. This is most conveniently done in the pressure cooker. After the cooker reaches maximum pressure, it takes 15-20 minutes, depending on the quality of the corn. Reserve the water in which the corn was boiled and remove the kernels from the ears. Keep aside.
2. In the pan, heat the oil. Add the cardamom

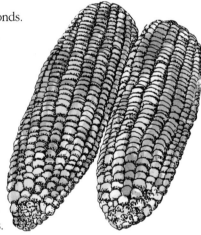

and fry a few seconds.
3. Add the cumin seeds and fry till they just change colour.
4. Add the onions and ginger and fry golden brown.
5. Add the salt, corn, capsicum, pepper and chilli. Fry a few seconds.
6. Add 4 cups of the liquid in which the corn was boiled, along with the rice. If the liquid falls short, add water to make it up to 4 cups. Raise heat till the liquid starts boiling and reaches the level of the rice, then reduce heat, cover the pan tightly, put the griddle underneath, weight it and cook 25-35 minutes.
7. Open the pan, check that the rice is cooked, then fluff up gently with the back of a spoon and serve, garnished if you like with crunchy, fried onions.

Serves 4.

NIMBU CHAWAL

*Lemon Rice.
A wholesome, lemony
speciality from the south.
Try it too when you want to
give leftover boiled rice a
totally new look
and flavour.*

INGREDIENTS

*2 cups rice, picked, washed and soaked in 4
cups water*
$^1/_2$ cup cooking oil
2 tablespoons unsalted peanuts
2 whole red chillies
A pinch of asafoetida
1 teaspoon mustard seeds
2 teaspoons white gram
1 teaspoon uncooked rice, picked
A few green chillies, deseeded and sliced
$^1/_2$ teaspoon turmeric powder
Juice of 4 limes
7-8 curry leaves, washed and torn up
1 tablespoon raisins
Salt to taste
1 tablespoon fresh, grated coconut

UTENSILS

A pan to boil the rice
A heavy-bottomed pan
Brown paper

Method

1. Boil the rice, (you can refer to the recipe for boiled rice). Keep aside.
2. While the rice is cooking, heat the oil and fry the peanuts golden brown. Remove from the oil and drain on the brown paper.
3. Strain the oil, leaving only 3-4 tablespoons in the pan. Heat it.
4. Drop in the red chillies. When they start to darken, add the asafoetida.
5. After another few seconds, add the mustard seeds, gram, and rice.
6. As soon as the seeds stop spluttering, add the rest of the ingredients, except the coconut. Be careful—the lime juice will splutter as you add it but it will subside in a few seconds.
7. Fluff up the rice and add to the pan. Stir to coat evenly. Add the peanuts.
8. Garnish with the coconut.

Serves 4.

DAHI CHAWAL

Rice with Curds.
A cooling meal that is often all you want to eat
in the hot summer months. You can put it together just before you eat.
If, however, you do it much in advance, you may keep it in the fridge,
but take it out before your meal because it does taste best eaten
at room temperature.

INGREDIENTS

2 cups rice, picked, washed and soaked in 4
cups water
2 cups fresh curds, lightly beaten
1-2 green chillies, deseeded and finely chopped
1-2 tablespoons fresh coriander, finely chopped
1 medium onion, finely chopped
A small piece of ginger, finely cubed (optional)
Salt to taste
1½ tablespoons cooking oil
½ teaspoon mustard seeds
1 teaspoon uncooked, picked rice
5-6 curry leaves, torn up

UTENSILS

A small, heavy-bottomed pan to cook the rice
Another bowl to mix all the ingredients
A small frying pan to make the tempering

Method

1. Boil the rice.

2. While the rice is still hot, mix in the curds. Use as much as needed, so that you get a result that is neither runny nor dry. The rice should be well coated.

3. Mix in the chillies, coriander, onion, ginger and salt.

4. In the frying pan, heat the oil. Drop in the mustard seeds and after a few seconds, the rice.

5. As soon as the seeds stop spluttering (you may need to cover the pan, so that you don't have flecks of oil all over yourself) drop in the curry leaves. After a second, pour the tempering over the rice. Mix in well and serve at room temperature.

Serves 4–6.

NARIYAL CHAWAL

Coconut Flavoured Rice.
Light, fresh-tasting and a
very pleasant change.

INGREDIENTS
1 large coconut
4 cups water
4-5 tablespoons cooking oil
4 onions, sliced
8-10 whole peppercorns
1 ½ teaspoon turmeric
Salt to taste
1 ½ tablespoons fresh coriander, finely chopped
(optional)
2 cups rice, picked, washed and soaked

UTENSILS
A heavy-bottomed pan with
a tight-fitting lid
A coconut scraper
An electric or manual grinder

Method

1. Break the coconut. Be careful not to waste the water. Keep it aside. Scrape the pulp out from the coconut. This is most conveniently done with a coconut scraper—a gadget that has a ball with serrated edges fixed on to a handle. The ball fits inside a half coconut and as you move the handle, the pulp is grated out. Over the pulp, pour 2 cups of the water, heated. Keep it aside for about half an hour, then blend well. Pour the paste into a strainer. Over it pour the coconut water and from the remaining 2 cups of water, as much as you need to make the total quantity 4 cups. Keep pressing down with a wooden or metal spoon to extract as much flavour and pulp as possible. What is left in the strainer may be discarded.

2. Heat the oil in the pan. Add half the sliced onions. Fry to a crisp, golden brown on high heat. Remove and keep aside. Into the same oil, add the peppercorns and after a few seconds, the rest of the onions. Fry golden brown.

3. Add the turmeric and salt.

4. After another few seconds, add the rice, coriander and coconut flavoured water. Stir well, cover the pan tightly and cook on high heat. When the water level reaches the level of the rice, reduce the heat, put a griddle underneath the pan and cook on a slow fire for 25 minutes. Open the pan, check that the rice is done and gently fluff up with the back of a spoon before serving, garnished with the crisp fried onions.

Serves 4.

IDLI

Steamed Rice Cakes.
A light, steamed speciality from the south.
Here is a recipe for it, perfected after many trials.
Idlis *are best served with coconut chutney*
and sambhar.

INGREDIENTS
3 cups idli rave *(special ground rice)*
*1 cup White Gram (*urad dal*) (husked)*
Water
2 teaspoons salt

UTENSILS
Two bowls to soak the rice and gram
Another large one to ferment the batter
An electric or manual grinder
An idli *mould*
A pressure cooker or large pan.

Method
1. The procedure for making *idlis* must start a whole 24 hours before you want to eat them. Pick, wash and soak the *rave* and *dal* separately in water. You can do this in the morning. At the end of the day, grind each with a little water. When you mix the two, the batter should look like a thick, slightly grainy custard that can be poured easily. Put it into the larger bowl, cover and leave to ferment for the whole night in a dry, warm place. By the next morning, it should have more than doubled in volume. Beat it vigorously with metal spoon or with your hand.
2. Lightly grease the *idli* moulds. This gadget, specially designed to steam *idlis*, is the best and most convenient way of making them. Branching out from a central rod are shallow, cup-shaped moulds, into which you will pour a tablespoon of the batter. It will rise slightly so leave some space for it. You may substitute with an egg-poacher.

3. Heat about 1 cup water in the cooker or pan. Check earlier that your mould fits easily into it. While the water is coming to the boil, ladle the batter into each mould. As soon as you notice that the steam has formed, gently ease the mould inside, cover the pan or cooker and keep 10-15 minutes. Check that the idlis are done by poking a tooth-pick in the centre of one, then take out the whole mould. Leave it to cool for about 5 minutes before gently easing out the idlis. You might need to push a spoon or blunt knife around the edges to loosen them. Serve immediately.

Makes about 30 idlis.

The best way to reheat left-over idlis *is to wrap them in foil and steam for a few minutes.*

43

SINDHI PULAO

Rice cooked in the Sindhi Style.
A quite differently made but equally flavourful meal.
It needs no accompaniments other than curds
and perhaps, a chutney.

INGREDIENTS

6 tablespoons cooking oil; 1 teaspoon cumin seeds, preferably black (shahzeera)
4 large onions, sliced; 500 gm meat, washed; ½ cup curds, lightly beaten; 1-1 ½ teaspoons whole black peppercorns, ground; 1 teaspoon coriander powder; ½ teaspoon turmeric powder; 2 bay leaves; Whole red chillies or chopped green chillies, to taste; Salt to taste; 8 green cardamoms, ground or pounded; 4-5 cloves, 2 pieces cinnamon; 2 black cardamoms; pounded; 1½ piece of ginger, cut in thin strips; 2 cups rice, picked, washed and soaked; A handful of almonds, blanched and lightly fried (optional)

UTENSILS

A pressure cooker; A heavy-bottomed pan with a tight fitting lid; A griddle; A weight

Method

1. In the pressure cooker, heat half the oil.
2. Drop in the cumin.
3. After a few seconds, add half the onions. Fry light brown.
4. Add the meat. After its juices dry up, fry till it just changes colour.
5. To the curds, add the next 6 ingredients. Mix well and add to the meat in the pan. Also add half a cup of water.
6. Close the cooker. Let it reach maximum pressure, then reduce heat and keep 5-7 minutes. Turn off the heat. Let the pressure reduce on its own. Open it and check that the meat is at least three-quarters tenderised and the gravy is thick. If necessary, let it boil for a few more minutes.
7. In a separate pan, heat the rest of the oil. Drop in the spices. Fry a few seconds.
8. Add the remaining onions. Fry light brown.
9. Add the strips of ginger. Fry another minute.
10. Add the rice. Don't throw away the water in which it was soaked. Fry the rice for a few minutes till it starts sticking to the bottom. Take off the fire and remove three-quarters of it from the pan. On top of the quarter left in, arrange a layer of meat. Continue layering, alternately, the rice and meat. Pour in water to come about one inch above the level of the meat and rice in the pan. Use the same water in which the rice was soaked.
11. Close the lid tightly. Raise the heat. As soon as the liquid boils and reaches the level of the rice, reduce heat, put the griddle underneath the pan, put the weight on to the lid and keep for 30 minutes, or till the rice is completely tenderised and all the excess liquids have evaporated. Mix gently.
12. Serve garnished with the almonds.

Serves 6.

YAKHNI PULLAO

Rice Cooked with Meat.
Such a flavourful recipe —
you will enjoy it.

INGREDIENTS

2 cups rice, picked and washed
500 gm meat, washed
5-6 small pieces cinnamon
15 cloves
25 whole black peppercorns
6 black cardamoms, pounded
4 cups water
Salt to taste
5 tablespoons cooking oil
4 large onions, sliced
2 tablespoons ginger, ground, and 2 teaspoons, chopped
3 tablespoons ground garlic
A few green chillies, whole or sliced
2 soup or stock cubes

UTENSILS

A pressure cooker
A heavy-bottomed pan with a tight-fitting lid
A griddle and a weight

Method

1. Soak the rice in water for about 1 hour before cooking.

2. Into the pressure cooker put the meat and the whole spices. Add the water and salt and close the cooker. Allow it to reach maximum pressure, then reduce heat and keep for 5 minutes. Turn off the heat. Let the pressure reduce by itself. Open the cooker, separate the meat from the stock and the whole spices. Discard the latter.

3. Heat the oil to smoking point. Reduce heat and add the onions. Fry till soft and just beginning to brown. Add half of the garlic and the ginger. Stirring continuously, fry till it starts to brown and stick to the bottom.

4. Add the meat and fry for 10-15 minutes. Add the chillies. Though you have to keep stirring, do it gently so the meat doesn't break.

5. Add the rest of the ginger and garlic and fry another 10 minutes.

6. Measure out the reserved liquid and if needed, add water to it to make it up to 4 cups. Add the stock cubes to it and pour it into the pan along with the rice. You can discard the water in which it was soaked. Stir, close the lid tightly and raise the heat. After the liquid starts boiling, keep on high heat till it reaches the level of the rice, then reduce heat, put the griddle underneath, the weight on top and cook tightly covered, for 30 minutes.

7. Open the pan, check that the rice is done, then gently fluff up with the back of a spoon. Serve immediately if possible otherwise keep covered on the hot griddle.

Serves 6.

KEEMA CHAWAL

*Rice with Minced Meat.
An interesting change in looks as well as taste,
from the normal meat* pullao. *For a real intermingling of flavours,
serve with a south Indian split red gram* dal *and Punjabi* raita.

INGREDIENTS

250 gms curds, lightly beaten
2 onions, ground
1" piece of ginger, ground
6 cloves garlic, ground
1 black cardamom, pounded
½ teaspoon turmeric powder
1 teaspoon cumin seeds, roasted and ground
1 teaspoon fennel seeds (sonf), whole
2 teaspoons coriander powder and salt to taste
500 gms mince, washed
6 tablespoons cooking oil
1 teaspoon cumin seeds
2 cups rice, picked, washed and soaked in 3 cups water
2 soup or stock cubes (chicken)
4 tablespoons fresh coriander
2 tablespoons fresh mint
Milk

UTENSILS

Pressure cooker
A heavy-bottomed pan with a tight-fitting lid
A griddle A weight
A bowl to marinate the mince in

Method

1. Into the curds, mix the eight ingredients which follow, and salt.

2. Marinate the meat in the curds and leave for a couple of hours.

3. Heat half the oil in the pressure cooker and turn the meat into the pan. When the liquids dry up, fry the meat to a rich brown.

4. Add 1 cup water. Close the cooker. After it reaches maximum pressure, reduce heat and keep on the fire 7-8 minutes. Open the cooker and if the mince is too liquidy, raise the heat and let some of the water evaporate. It should ideally look like a thick sauce.

5. In a separate pan, heat the remaining oil. Drop in the cumin and let it darken slightly.

6. Add the rice, with the water in which it was soaked, the soup cubes, the coriander, mint and salt. Cover the pan, raise the heat and let the water reach the level of the rice. Reduce heat and cook till the water has evaporated. This should take about 10 minutes in which time, the rice should be about half-cooked.

7. In a large pan, layer the rice and minced meat. Sprinkle some milk over each layer.

8. Put the pan on the fire. As soon as steam begins to form, put the griddle underneath, the weight on top and keep on *dum* for at least half an hour.

9. Mix together well before serving.

Serves 6.

MANY FLAVOURED
PULSES

DALS

Pulses

While we were living abroad, a young Indian couple visiting the city, literally invited themselves over for dinner one evening. "Don't cook anything fancy, please," the man said, "just some *dal–roti*". A minute later, almost as if to justify his desperation, he added apologetically. "You know, one just doesn't realise the power of *dal* over an Indian until one is far away from home." Many times, in the fifteen years since he made that remark, I have found myself thinking how right he was.

When we are at home, planning our daily menus, we reach for that jar of *dal* on an almost daily basis. It could be a simple Split Green Gram (*Mung*) today, a mixture of it and Lentils (*Masoor*) for a change; you could opt for a rich Black Gram (*Sabut Maa*) that will need more than an hour to simmer to perfection or you could decide to make an interesting blend of more than one kind. Alternately, you can try the same *dal* with a different tempering, for a complete change in flavour—mustard seeds, for example, instead of cumin; browned onions to add a unique flavour; a sprinkling of dill, perhaps or a pinch of aromatic asafoetida. There are just so many variations. You will find some in this section. I have tried to make them as diversely–flavoured as possible.

The first recipe is one for a Split Green Gram, perhaps the quickest *dal* to cook but also one that you have to be careful with since you can quite easily reduce it to an overcooked hash.

Also, you can just as easily smother its delicate flavour with too much spice. I prefer it flavoured simply with a gentle tempering. Talking of temperings, see how the second recipe uses asafoetida and curds to completely transform this same *dal* into a quite different preparation, in looks, flavour and even colour. The recipe illustrates well the magical adaptability of the same *dal*, and this holds true for most varieties. Further on in the section, you have the famous Punjabi *Makhani Dal*, literally buttery *dal*, a name which hints at its richness. It is cooked with curds and butter, tempered with cinnamon, and garnished with refreshing, fresh coriander. It is party fare alright, as royal as the last *dal* is homely. Aside from other variations from different parts of the country, you will find two *Kadhis*, best described for someone unfamiliar to Indian cuisine, as creamy, thick, soup like preparations, usually served with boiled rice. Not *dals* in the strict sense, both incorporate gramflour though one is a curd-based recipe while the other bursts with vegetables, and the piquant flavour of tamarind.

And then, there are the beans of course—the red Kidney Beans (*Rajmah*) curried and Chick–peas (*channa*) in a typical, spicy but dry preparation. There is a dry *dal* too, and to complete the picture, two distinctive recipes that introduce you to yet another facet of these fascinating pulses. In these, the *dals* are ground, shaped into balls, fried and then cooked in a complimentary curry. They make an interesting addition to any menu.

What you will not find here are the other preparations that *dals* play an equally important role in—*dosas, idlis* and *vadas, halwas* and vegetables and meats cooked with *dals*. Look for them in the relevant sections and I am sure you will find yourself agreeing that *dals* do, indeed, have some indefinable (or should that read definable?) power over the Indian palate. I must add here that apart from the varied ways in which they are used in our cuisine, *dals* do indeed boast an impressive bio–data. They are very rich sources of proteins and many nutrients among them iron, thiamin, riboflavin, potassium, phosphorous. They are good sources of fibre and yes, they are cholesterol–free. Are you wondering where the catch is? Well, there isn't really any except that some of these powerful proteins often cause flatulence. The Black Gram is one example. Bengal Gram is another culprit. Chick–peas and Kidney–Beans too are not blameless. But this is not a cause for despair— ginger is an effective antidote. You will find it included in the recipes and you can also munch some more on the side (see the recipe for the ginger relish) to enjoy your *dal* without the discomfort!

Before we go on to the recipes, a few tips on dealing with *dals*: all of them need to be picked before cooking. In some cases, for example, the Black Gram, special vigilance is needed to weed out the little black stones that are often quite indistinguishable from the *dal* itself. After picking, the *dal* must be washed in a couple of changes of water after which it is left, like rice, to soak, usually for about half an hour before cooking. This cuts down on cooking time. Some, of course, are more fussy, and enjoy sitting in the water overnight. You will find instructions in the relevant recipes. Preferably soak in clean water because you will use the same to cook the *dal* in. If you are using the pressure cooker, which cuts down immeasurably on cooking time, you could add a little oil to the *dal* while it's boiling to minimise the risk of the *dal* sticking or causing pressure–cooker accidents. Particularly with pressure–cooking, in which the process is quick but doesn't allow you a peek to see exactly what's happening, it's a good idea to measure out water and keep an accurate track of time to ensure palatable and consistent results. In case you prefer not to pressure cook, use more water (a little less than double the quantity) since the *dals* will need a considerably longer time to tenderise. In that case, you would do well to use any heavy-bottomed pan. Another thing you should keep in mind: if you make the *dal* much in advance of serving time, it will thicken as it sits. This differs from *dal* to *dal* but happens to a greater or lesser degree in each case. You might have to add a little hot water to it when you finally heat it up to bring it back to the consistency you want.

Let's get down to savouring them then, these powerful, protein–rich pulses in all their varied flavours and colours.

MOONG DAL 1

Split Green Gram.
The quickest to cook, the
most easily digestible and if
its delicate flavour is not
smothered , delicious.

INGREDIENTS
$^1/_2$ *cup Split Green Gram, picked, washed and*
soaked in 4 cups water
1 onion, chopped fine
1" piece of ginger, chopped in minute cubes
1–2 green chillies, deseeded and chopped
$^1/_4$ *teaspoon turmeric powder*
Salt to taste
2 tablespoons butter, ghee or oil
1 teaspoon cumin
2 small tomatoes, chopped
1 tablespoon fresh coriander, chopped

UTENSILS
A pressure cooker
A small pan to make the tempering

Method

1. Boil the *dal* in the water in which it was
soaked with the next five ingredients. In the
pressure cooker, this will take just 3–4 minutes
after the cooker reaches maximum pressure. If
you decide not to pressure cook, boil till the *dal*
is soft and well–blended. This will take between
10 and 15 minutes.
2. Heat the oil, butter or *ghee*. Add the cumin.
Before it gets too dark, add the tomatoes. Cook
till the fat separates.
3. Add this tempering to the *dal* and stir well.
4. Garnish with the coriander before serving.

Serves 4.

Note: This dal *permits many variations. If you*
don't want to add the ginger and onion to it
while it's cooking, you can fry it in the
tempering (after the cumin) for a quite
different flavour and look.

If you do not wish to pressure cook, see
additional instructions in the introduction to
this section.

MOONG DAL 2

*Split Green Gram.
This recipe is a good example
of a humble dal that can be
made quite unusual. I first
tasted this variation at a
Kashmiri friend's house.*

INGREDIENTS

$^1/_2$ *cup* dal, *picked, washed and soaked in 4
cups water.*
A few green chillies, chopped fine
$^1/_2$ *teaspoon turmeric powder*
Salt to taste
1 cup curds
2 tablespoons oil or ghee
A pinch of asafoetida
Sugar to taste

UTENSILS

A pressure cooker
A small pan to make the tempering

Method

1. Boil the *dal* in the
water in which it was
soaked along with
the next three

ingredients. In the pressure cooker it shouldn't
take more than 3–4 minutes after the cooker
reaches maximum pressure. Open the cooker and
check that the *dal* is tenderised and well–
blended, though not completely mashed.
2. Lightly beat the curds. Stirring continuously,
add to the *dal.* Simmer a few minutes.
3. Meanwhile, make the tempering. Heat the
oil or *ghee.* Add the asafoetida. As soon as it
darkens, add the tempering to the *dal.*
Simmer another minute before taking off
the fire.
4. Check the seasoning. Add a little sugar if
needed, before serving.

Serves 4.

*If you do not wish to pressure cook, see
additional instructions in the introduction to
this section.*

MAKHANI
DAL

Whole Black Gram.
This dal *is as rich as the last is simple.*
Cooked to perfection, this speciality from
the north should be thickish, creamy and
very flavourful.

INGREDIENTS

1 cup Black Gram, picked, washed, and
soaked overnight
1 handful chickpeas, picked, washed and
soaked along with the gram
1 handful kidney beans, picked, washed and
soaked along with the gram
2 onions, finely chopped
8–10 cloves garlic, finely chopped
1" piece of ginger, chopped or sliced

Green chillies to taste, chopped or whole
$^1/_2$ teaspoon turmeric
Salt to taste
3 tablespoons cream, lightly beaten
4 tablespoons curds, lightly beaten
2 tablespoons fresh, chopped coriander
$1^1/_2$ teaspoons ground cumin
2 tablespoons butter or ghee
$^1/_2$ teaspoon ground cumin
1" piece of ginger, cut in thin sticks
$^1/_2$ teaspoon ground cinnamon
2 small tomatoes, chopped

UTENSILS
A pressure cooker
A small pan to make the
tempering

Method

1. Put the first nine ingredients into the pressure cooker. Add 6 cups water, including that in which the *dal* was soaked. Close the cooker and allow it to come to maximum pressure. Reduce heat and cook 35 minutes.
2. Open the cooker, check that the gram is tender and well blended then add the cream, curds, coriander and cumin. Cover and simmer another 30 minutes, stirring every once in a while.
3. In a small pan, heat the butter or *ghee*. Add the cumin and after a few seconds, the ginger. Fry lightly.
4. Add the cinnamon and tomatoes. Cook till the fat separates. Add to the *dal*. Simmer 5 minutes before serving.

Serves 6–8.

Note: This dal *can be frozen successfully. If you intend to do that, however, cook it till stage 1 only, i.e., don't add the curds and cream.*
If you do not wish to pressure cook, see additional instructions in the introduction to this section.

DAL PANCHRATAN

Mixed Pulses.
This dal *is jokingly referred to in our family*
as langar dal. *According to my father, who*
served in the army, it is the one most
commonly served in the langar *(common*
canteen for soldiers) because into it you can
conveniently throw in whatever is available.

INGREDIENTS

$^1/_2$ *cup Bengal Gram, picked, washed and*
soaked in $5^1/_2$ *cups of water*

$^1/_2$ *cup Black Gram, picked, washed and soaked*
in the same water

$^1/_2$ *cup Red Gram, picked, washed and soaked*
in the same water

$^1/_2$ *cup Lentils, picked, washed and soaked in*
the same water

$^1/_2$ *cup Split Green Gram, picked, washed and*
soaked in the same water

4 tablespoons ghee *or oil; 2 small onions,*
sliced; 2 small onions, ground; 5 cloves garlic,
ground; $1^1/_2$*" piece of ginger, ground; 1 teaspoon*
coriander powder; $^1/_2$ *teaspoon turmeric powder,*
green chillies, chopped or red chilli powder,
to taste; Salt to taste

$^1/_2$ *teaspoon* garam masala *powder*

Juice of half a lime

$1^1/_2$ *tablespoons fresh coriander, chopped*

UTENSILS

A pressure cooker

A small pan to make the tempering

Method

1. Heat the oil or *ghee.* Add the sliced onions. Fry golden brown.

2. Add the next six ingredients, i.e., from the onion to the chilli. Keep stirring and frying, adding a few drops of water if necessary, till the fat separates, and the mixture is a rich brown.

3. Add the *dals* along with the water in which they were soaked and salt. Close the cooker and allow it to come to maximum pressure. Reduce heat and keep on the fire about 14 minutes. Open the cooker and check that each *dal* is tenderised and the whole is well–blended. Boil away any excess water.

4. Stir in the *garam masala,* lime juice and coriander before serving.

Serves 8-10.

If you do not wish to pressure cook, see additional instructions in the introduction to this section.

CHANNE KI DAL 1

Bengal Gram.
Though flavoured differently in
different parts of the country, as you
will notice in the next recipe, this dal
is popular all over and rightly so. It
does have a very wholesome flavour.

INGREDIENTS

1 cup Bengal Gram soaked in 3 cups water
$^1/_2$ teaspoon turmeric powder
Salt to taste
Green chillies to taste, chopped
2 tablespoons oil
$^1/_2$ teaspoon cumin seeds
2 small onions, sliced
1" piece ginger, cubed or cut in strips.
2 small tomatoes, chopped
$^1/_4 - ^1/_2$ teaspoon dried fenugreek

UTENSILS
A pressure cooker
A small pan for making the tempering

Method

1. Put the *dal*, along with the water in which it was soaked, the turmeric, salt, and green chillies into the cooker. Close the cooker and allow it to reach maximum pressure. Reduce heat and keep about 10 minutes. If you have time, let the pressure reduce by itself. The *dal* should have soaked up the water but it should not be broken or mashed. Boil away any excess water.

2. Heat the oil. Drop in the cumin seeds.

3. After a few seconds, add the onions. Fry light brown.

4. Add the ginger. Fry onions and ginger golden brown.

5. Add the tomatoes and fenugreek. Fry till the fat separates. Turn into the *dal*. Simmer 5 minutes before serving.

Serves 4–6.

Note: For a change you can add ground garlic and ginger to the dal *while it's cooking. In that case, omit ginger from the tempering.*
If you do not wish to pressure cook, see additional instructions in the introduction to this section.

CHANNE KI DAL 2

Bengal Gram Bengali Style.
The same dal *but with a*
different flavour. Try both.

INGREDIENTS

1 cup Bengal Gram, soaked in 3 cups water
Salt to taste
$\frac{1}{2}$ teaspoon turmeric powder
$\frac{1}{2}$ teaspoon sugar
3 cloves
2 green cardamoms, pounded roughly
A small piece cinnamon
$1\frac{1}{2}$ tablespoons oil
$\frac{1}{2}$ teaspoon cumin seeds
2 red chillies, broken and deseeded
1" piece ginger, cubed or cut in strips
1 tablespoon coconut powder
or fresh, grated coconut

UTENSILS

A pressure cooker
A small pan for making the tempering

Method

1. Put the *dal*, along with the water, salt, turmeric, sugar, cloves, cardamon and cinnamon into the cooker. Allow it to come to maximum pressure. Reduce heat and keep for 10 minutes. If you have time, let the pressure reduce by itself.
2. Heat the oil. Drop in the cumin and chillies.
3. After a few seconds, add the ginger. Fry a few seconds, then turn into the *dal*. Stir in well. Simmer 5 minutes.
4. Add the coconut. Stir well before serving.

Serves 4.

Note: This dal cooks with the grains visible. If you want a smoother result, add a little more water (about $\frac{1}{2}$ cup) and cook 8 minutes extra. For a really smooth dal, blend it with a wooden masher.
If you do not wish to pressure cook, see additional instructions in the introduction to this section.

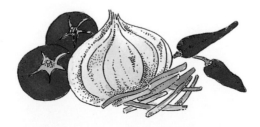

SAMBHAR

Split Red Gram.
The famous dal *of the south, piquant and*
appetising. Add as many or as few vegetables as you
like and you have a wholesome accompaniment to
rice. The plain, boiled one goes best with this.

INGREDIENTS

1 cup Split Red Gram, picked, washed and
soaked in 4 cups water; A few curry leaves,
washed and torn up; ¹/₂ teaspoon turmeric
powder; Salt and red chilli powder to taste;
2¹/₂ tablespoons cooking oil; 1 whole, red chilli;
A pinch of asafoetida; 1 teaspoon mustard
seeds; 1 teaspoon fenugreek seeds; 1 teaspoon
uncooked rice, picked; 1 large onion, chopped;
2 cups mixed vegetables, washed and chopped;
1¹/₂ teaspoons sambhar *powder; 2 tomatoes; 1–2*
tablespoons tamarind, soaked in ¹/₂ cup water;
1 teaspoon sugar (optional)

UTENSILS
A pressure cooker
A heavy–bottomed pan with a lid

Method
1. Put the *dal* along with the water in which it
was soaked and the curry leaves, turmeric
powder, chillies and salt into the pressure
cooker. Close the cooker and allow it to come to
maximum pressure. Reduce heat and keep on
the fire 10–12 minutes. If you have time, allow
the pressure to reduce by itself.
2. In the other pan, heat the oil. Drop in the
chilli. As soon as it darkens, remove and discard.
3. Drop in the asafoetida. In a few seconds, it

will change colour.
4. Drop the seeds into the pan. Cover it to avoid
messy spluttering.
5. As soon as the seeds stop spluttering, add the
rice. In a few seconds, it will brown.
6. Add the onion. Fry light brown.
7. Add the vegetables. Start by adding those
which take longer to cook, and when they are
parboiled, you can add the quicker cooking
ones.
8. Add the *sambhar* powder and the tomatoes.
Add water if needed, to tenderise the vegetables.
Cover and cook till they're all tenderised.
9. Through a strainer, squeeze the tamarind pulp
and the water in which it was soaked. Discard the
seeds and pour the water into the pot of vegetables. Bring to boil and simmer 3-4 minutes.
10. Add the *dal* to the vegetables. Stir well and
simmer together for ten minutes before serving.
Taste and adjust seasoning, adding the sugar if
required.

Serves 4–6.

Note: You can cook this dal *without vegetables*
too if you prefer. Just leave out step 7. If you
do not wish to pressure cook, see additional
instructions in the introduction to this section.

GUJARATI DAL

Split Red Gram.
The typical Gujarati dal. *The last recipe—*
sambhar—*uses the same* dal *but see how*
different it can taste.

INGREDIENTS

1 cup Split Red Gram, picked, washed and soaked in 4 cups water

Salt to taste

½ teaspoon turmeric powder

2 tablespoons cooking oil

½ teaspoon mustard seeds

½ teaspoon cumin seeds

A pinch of asafoetida

Green chillies to taste, chopped

1 tomato, chopped

10 cocums

A small piece of jaggery

1–2 tablespoons coconut, grated (optional)

A few curry leaves

1 tablespoon finely chopped ginger

UTENSILS

A pressure cooker

A small pan

Method

1. Put the *dal* along with the water in which it was soaked, the salt, and turmeric into the cooker. Close the cooker and allow it to come to maximum pressure. Reduce heat and keep on the fire 10–12 minutes. If you have time, allow the pressure to reduce by itself.

2. In the small pan, heat the oil. Drop in the mustard seeds, followed by the cumin and finally, the asafoetida. As soon as the seeds stop spluttering, turn into the *dal*. Let it come to a simmer.

3. Add the rest of the ingredients and simmer another ten minutes before serving.

Serves 4.

Note: If you do not wish to pressure cook, see additional instructions in the introduction to this section.

62

SABUT MASUR DAL

Whole Lentils.
This is the whole version of the salmon–coloured lentils. This cooks
into a brown coloured dal *and this is a very special recipe for it*
with, as you will notice, an unusual tempering, that hails from
the Kumaon hills.

INGREDIENTS

1 cup Lentils, washed and soaked in 5 cups water
Salt to taste
Green chillies to taste, chopped or red chilli powder
$\frac{1}{2}$ teaspoon turmeric powder
3 teaspoons mustard seeds
$1\frac{1}{2}$ teaspoons cumin seeds
12 cloves garlic
2 tablespoons oil
2 onions, sliced
2 tomatoes, chopped
2 tablespoons tamarind, soaked in $\frac{1}{2}$ cup water
$1\frac{1}{2}$ tablespoons fresh coriander, finely chopped

UTENSILS

A pressure cooker
An electric blender or manual grinder
A small pan to make the tempering
A strainer

Method

1. Put the *dal* along with the water, salt, chillies and turmeric into the pressure cooker. Allow it to come to maximum pressure then reduce heat and keep 12 minutes. Let the pressure reduce by itself. Open the cooker and check that the *dal* is well blended and tenderised. Boil away any excess water.

2. While the *dal* is boiling, grind together the mustard seeds, cumin seeds and garlic. This is easiest done in an electric blender but you can also do it manually.

3. To make the tempering, heat the oil. Add the onions. Fry golden brown.

4. Add the ground paste. Fry another few seconds stirring continuously.

5. Add the tomatoes. Fry till the fat separates.

6. Strain the tamarind water, and push through the strainer as much of the pulp as you can. Discard the seeds. Add the tamarind to the pan. Let it come to a boil. Simmer a few minutes, and garnish with the coriander before serving.

Serves 6.

If you do not wish to pressure cook, see additional instructions in the introduction to this section.

RAJMAH

Curried Kidney Beans.
Served with rice, rajmah *makes a*
very popular menu, specially
with children.

INGREDIENTS
$1^1/_2$ *cups* Rajmah *picked, washed and soaked*
overnight
5 tablespoons cooking oil
1 large black cardamom, pounded
3 onions, ground
$1^1/_2$ *teaspoons ground ginger*
1 teaspoon ground garlic
2 large tomatoes, pureed or blanched and
chopped
Green chillies to taste, chopped
1 teaspoon coriander powder
1 teaspoon cumin powder
$^1/_2$ *teaspoon turmeric powder*
Salt to taste
1 tablespoon fresh coriander, chopped.

UTENSILS
A pressure cooker

Method
1. Heat the oil. Drop in the cardamom. Let it
sizzle for a minute.
2. Add the onions. Fry light brown.
3. Add the ginger and garlic. Stir and fry till
golden brown. You may need to add a few
teaspoons water if it starts sticking too much to
the bottom of the pan.
4. Add the tomatoes, and chillies. Fry till the fat
separates.
5. Add the rest of the ingredients except the
fresh coriander. Stir and fry a minute or two.
6. Add the beans without the water. Mix well
with the contents of the cooker and fry till the
beans change colour and darken.
7. Add the water—you can use the water in
which the *rajmah* was soaked. First
add just as much as you need to make the
curry the consistency you desire then add
$1^1/_4$ cups extra, which will evaporate during
cooking.
8. Close the cooker and allow it to reach
maximum pressure. Reduce heat and cook 45
minutes. Take off the fire and if you have time,
let the pressure reduce by itself. Open the
cooker, check that the *rajmah* has tenderised
and the curry is the consistency you want. Boil
some more if necessary.
9. Serve garnished with fresh coriander. This
dish goes best with boiled rice.

Serves 4–6.

Rajasthani Dal

Pulses Cooked in the Rajasthani style.
An interesting blend of flavours. I
picked up this recipe from one of the
erstwhile royal kitchens—Samode.

INGREDIENTS

$^1/_2$ *cup Bengal Gram, picked, washed and*
soaked, in 2 cups water
$^1/_2$ *cup White Gram, picked, washed and soaked*
in 2 cups water
$^1/_2$ *cup Green Gram, picked, washed and*
soaked in 2 cups water
$^1/_2$ *teaspoon turmeric powder*
1" piece of ginger, minutely cubed
1 onion, finely chopped
2 cloves
2 small sticks cinnamon
Salt to taste
Red chilli powder, to taste
2 tablespoons oil or ghee
1 teaspoon cumin seeds
1–2 tablespoons fresh coriander, chopped

UTENSILS

A pressure cooker

A small pan to make the tempering

Method

1. Put all the *dals*, along with the water in
which they were soaked into the pressure cooker
along with the next seven ingredients. After the
cooker reaches maximum pressure, reduce heat
and keep about 15 minutes. Open the cooker and
check that the *dal* has
tenderised and is well–blended. Boil away any
excess water.
2. In the small pan, heat the oil or *ghee*.
Add the cumin. As soon as it starts to darken, add
to the *dal*.
3. Serve garnished with the fresh coriander.

Serves 6-8.

If you do not wish to pressure cook, see additional
instructions in the introduction to
this section.

CHATPATE CHANNE

Spicy Chickpeas.
Spicy, simple to make, these
chickpeas are irresistible.

INGREDIENTS

500 gms (just over 2$\frac{1}{2}$ cups) chickpeas, picked,
washed and soaked overnight
A pinch of baking soda
1 teaspoon oil
Salt to taste
50 grams pomegranate seeds (anardana)
2 tablespoons oil
1" piece of ginger, cut in fine strips
Whole green chillies
3 tablespoons ghee *or oil*
2–3 teaspoons freshly ground garam masala
(see Glossary)

UTENSILS

A pressure cooker
A small pan to fry the ginger and chillies
An electric or manual grinder
A griddle or small heavy bottomed pan

Method

1. Put the chickpeas along with the baking soda,
1 teaspoon oil and salt into the
cooker. From the water in which the chickpeas
were soaked, add only as much as just covers
them in the cooker. Close the cooker and put on
the fire. After it reaches maximum pressure,
reduce heat and keep just 7–9 minutes. Open

and check that they're tenderised. They
must not be mashed or overdone. Remove
from the cooker, drain any excess water and
keep aside.

2. While the chickpeas are boiling, roast the
pomegranate seeds. This is best done on a
griddle or in a small, heavy–bottomed pan. They
will turn dark and aromatic. Take them off the
fire, let them cool then grind them as finely as
possible. Keep aside.

3. Put the 2 tablespoons of oil in a pan. Fry the
strips of ginger till they're lightly browned and
starting to wrinkle. Do the same to the chillies.
Remove them from the oil. Keep the oil aside too
to reuse.

4. When you're ready to serve, boil the *ghee* or
oil. *Ghee* is traditionally used. Pour it over the
chickpeas. Also sprinkle over the garam masala
and pomegranate seeds. Shake the pan gently to
coat the chickpeas evenly.

5. Serve garnished with the fried ginger and
green chillies.

Serves 6–8.

Note: Remember that if you do not presoak the
peas, they will take longer to cook. You may also
use cooked, canned ones if you like.

PUNJABI KADHI

A curd-gramflour speciality.
This curd–rich, creamy kadhi, *which takes over an hour to simmer to perfection, and fills the house with appetising aromas while it's doing so, is a delicious indulgence, specially on a lazy Sunday afternoon. This is the way it's normally made in Punjab.*

INGREDIENTS

For the kadhi
2 cups curds, lightly beaten; 6 cups water
1 cup gramflour; ¹/₂ teaspoon turmeric powder;
Salt to taste; 6–7 curry leaves, torn up;
1–2 green chillies, deseeded and sliced
For the tempering
2 tablespoons oil; A large pinch of asafoetida;
1–2 whole red chillies; teaspoon aniseed; ¹/₂
teaspoon cumin; ¹/₂ teaspoon fenugreek seeds; ¹/₂
teaspoon mustard seeds; ¹/₂ teaspoon dried
fenugreek; 1 teaspoon sugar or a small piece of
jaggery
For the Dumplings
Oil for frying; 1 cup gramflour; ¹/₂ cup curds; 1
small onion, finely chopped; 1 green chilli,
finely chopped; ¹/₂ teaspoon pomegranate seeds,
crushed; Salt to taste

UTENSILS

A large, heavy–bottomed pan with a lid
Another pan to fry the dumplings
2 small bowls
Brown paper

Method

1. Mix together the water and curds and stir in the gram flour, making sure there are no lumps.
2. Add to it the turmeric, salt, curry leaves and chillies. Cover and cook on a slow fire till the mixture is creamy, thickened and reduced by about half.
3. While the *kadhi* is cooking, you can make the dumplings. In a pan, heat the oil to almost smoking point.
4. Mix together all the ingredients for the dumplings. Beat well to ensure you have a smooth batter. Drop by spoonfuls into the hot oil, and fry to a golden brown. Drain on brown paper. Keep aside and add to the *kadhi* just a little while before serving.
5. To make the tempering, heat the oil. Drop in the asafoetida and the chillies.
6. After a few seconds, add all the seeds.
7. As soon as the seeds stop spluttering, add the fenugreek and immediately turn the tempering into the *kadhi*.
8. Check seasoning and add the jaggery or sugar if needed.

Serves 4.

SINDHI KADHI

A delicious Sindhi speciality.
Quite different from the last recipe, this is
a Sindhi recipe of a kadhi *bursting with*
vegetables and gramflour. It's best served
with boiled rice.

INGREDIENTS
5 tablespoons cooking oil
A pinch of asafoetida
Green chillies to taste, sliced
1 teaspoon fenugreek seeds
1 teaspoon cumin seeds
6 heaped tablespoons gramflour
1 sprig curry leaves
Salt to taste
1 teaspoon coriander powder
$\frac{1}{2}$ teaspoon turmeric powder
1 teaspoon cumin powder
2 cups mixed vegetables, including drumsticks,
if available
2 tablespoons tamarind, soaked in $\frac{1}{2}$ cup water
1-2 teaspoons sugar
1 tablespoon fresh coriander leaves, chopped

UTENSILS
A heavy-bottomed pan with a lid

Method

1. Heat the oil. Drop in the asafoetida. In a few seconds, it will change colour.

2. Add the chillies and seeds. Let them stop spluttering.

3. Add the gramflour. Stirring almost continuously, fry till the flour is lightly browned and very aromatic.

4. Take the pan off the fire and let it cool for about 10 minutes.

5. Add 5$\frac{1}{2}$ cups water. You must keep stirring continuously to avoid the formation of any lumps. The consistency should be of a fairly thin curry.

6. Put it back on the fire and add to it the curry leaves, salt, coriander, turmeric and cumin. Bring to boil.

7. Reduce heat and drop in the vegetables—if there are some that cook considerably slower than others, drop them in first. Cover the pan and let the *kadhi* simmer till it is slightly thickened and the vegetables are tenderised.

8. Push the tamarind pulp and water through a sieve or strainer, discarding the seeds. Add to the *kadhi* and boil for 2–3 minutes.

9. Check seasoning and add the sugar if needed.

10. Before serving, garnish with the coriander leaves.

Serves 6.

Note: What's magical about this Kadhi *is how it can be transformed by adding different combinations of vegetables. Use whichever ones are in season.*

SOOKHA DAL

*Dry White Gram.
A delicious recipe which takes
some practice to cook to perfection.*

INGREDIENTS

*1 cup White Gram soaked in 2 cups water
4 tablespoons cooking oil
2" piece of ginger, cut in strips
A few fresh green chillies*

*3 onions, sliced finely
$^1/_2$ teaspoon garam masala (See Glossary)
Juice of 1 lime*

UTENSILS

*A pan to boil the dal
A deep pan*

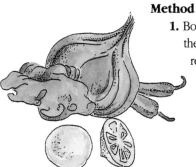

Method

1. Boil the *dal*. This is the secret of this recipe—the *dal* must be cooked just right—not undercooked, and certainly not mashed.

2. In the deep pan, heat the oil. Drop in the ginger slices. Fry till lightly browned. Remove and keep aside.

3. Into the same oil, drop the chillies. It's a good idea to make a small slit in the side of each so they don't burst. Fry till they're just starting to change colour. Remove from the oil and keep aside.

4. Into the same oil (add more if needed), put the onions. Fry golden brown. Turn the *dal* into the deep pan. Stir gently.

5. Sprinkle over the *garam masala* and stir in the lime juice.

6. Serve garnished with the strips of ginger and the green chillies.

Serves 4.

Note: Bengal Gram and Split Green Gram can also be cooked dry and used not only as an accompaniment at a meal but also as a stuffing for parathas.

70

DAL KOFTA CURRY

Fritters in Curry.
That's a rather staid name for a quite unusual
curry. Vegetarians are pleasantly surprised to be
told they can help themselves to it, too.

INGREDIENTS
250 gms Whole Lentils picked, washed and
soaked overnight
2" piece of ginger, chopped
12–15 cloves garlic
10 peppercorns
4 green cardamoms
2 cloves
A small stick of cinnamon
1 teaspoon coriander
Salt and red or green chillies to taste
2 tablespoons cooking oil
1 slice of bread
Oil for frying

UTENSILS
An electric or manual grinder
A deep pan
Brown paper

Method
1. Drain the Lentils and grind with the next eight ingredients. You can add a little water if you need. This is easiest done in an electric grinder but you can use a manual one if you like. You will have a thick, brownish paste.
2. Heat the oil gently in the pan. Turn the paste into it. It will bind and you may find it a little

difficult to stir. Do it as well as possible. When it is heated through, take off the fire.
3. Soak the bread for a few seconds in a little water then squeeze it out as thoroughly as possible. Crumble over the hot *kofta* mixture. Mix in thoroughly.
4. With greased palms, shape the *koftas*, as soon as the mixture is cool enough to handle. Don't leave it lying too long—it tends to get too crumbly and dry. You can make the *koftas* round or sausage–shaped.
5. Heat the oil for frying. You have to deep–fry so put in at least half a panful. When it's well–heated, slip in the *koftas*. Fry on gentle heat till browned evenly. Drain on brown paper.
6. Make the cream-tomato curry as in the recipe for *Shahi Paneer*. Just a little while before you're ready to serve, slip the *koftas* in and heat through. You can of course make any other curry of your choice for a change in flavour, though this particular tomato one does comple-ment the taste of the *koftas* very well.

Makes about 25 lemon-sized koftas.

Note: You can also make this as a snack, i.e., fry the koftas *and serve immediately with a chutney or tomato sauce.*

PAKORI SABZI

Such a refreshing change when you can't think of a supplement to your meal. It's popular and quite easy to put together.

INGREDIENTS

For the Fritters:
125 gms gramflour
1 onion, finely chopped
Green chillies to taste, finely chopped
A few teaspoons fresh coriander, finely chopped
A pinch of baking soda
I teaspoon pomegranate seeds, crushed (optional)
Salt to taste
Water
Oil for frying
For the Curry:
3 tablespoons cooking oil
Green chillies to taste, finely chopped
2 small onions, chopped or ground
1" piece of ginger, minutely cubed
2 small tomatoes, pureed or chopped
A pinch of turmeric powder
$^1/_2$ teaspoon coriander powder
Salt to taste

UTENSILS

A pan to make the batter
A deep pan to fry the fritters
A heavy-bottomed pan with a lid
Brown paper

Method

1. To make the fritters, mix all the ingredients except the oil with just as much water as is needed to make a thick batter with a dropping consistency. You have to stir vigorously to ensure it is absolutely smooth. Keep aside for 15 minutes.

2. In the deep pan, heat the oil. You have to deep-fry so you will need at least half a panful. When the oil is medium hot, drop in the first batch of fritters. You can do this by hand or with the help of two spoons. Fry golden brown. Check that they are cooked through. If they are beginning to burn or darken without cooking inside, the oil is too hot. Lower the heat, and wait a while before frying the next batch. Use up all the batter. Drain the fritters on brown paper.

3. To make the curry, heat the oil. Drop in the green chillies. Don't allow them to darken.

4. Add the onions. Fry light brown.

5. Add the ginger. Fry golden brown.

6. Add the tomatoes and spices. Fry till the fat separates.

7. Add water to make the curry a little thinner than you eventually want it to be. Simmer 5 minutes.

8. When you're ready to eat, heat the curry through, drop in the fritters and simmer 5-7 minutes. The curry will thicken considerably since the fritters will soak it up.
Serves 4-6.

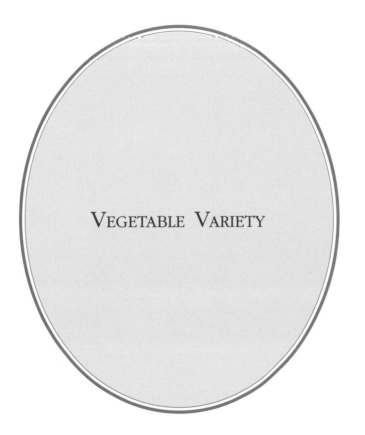

VEGETABLE VARIETY

VEGETABLE VARIETY

Foreigners who have never had the opportunity of visiting India often ask me about vegetarianism. Quite incredulously, they ask me to reconfirm that some Indians never, no never eat meat, not in any form, not even if there's nothing else to eat! Apart from the other reasons, I try to explain that it's easy to be a vegetarian in our country. We have such a wealth and variety of vegetables and such a wealth and variety of ways in which they can be savoured. The seasons are obliging too, kaleidoscopically changing the patterns we see on the stalls and carts with every turn of the weather. The green of peas, spinach and fenugreek, the snowy white of the cauliflower, the orange splash of the carrot slowly gives way to the pastels of the squashes, the gourds, the pumpkins and cucumber as summer takes over from winter. The colours of corn dominate the picture when the rains beat down while the perennial beige of the potato and ginger, the

bright red of the tomato and the fresh green of the chilli and coriander provide the touches of continuity, as the seasonal cycle gradually comes full circle again.

It is still a way of life in our country to buy freshly picked vegetables; to examine many potentials for juiciness, plumpness and good health before deciding which one to take home. When the meal is being planned, a *dal* supplements the green of the day; rice or *rotis* are taken-for-granted of course and some curds and relishes provide cooling, piquant counter-points. You have a healthy, balanced menu in which a meat is far from indispensable.

Apart from the tempting choice of vegetables available, our cuisine offers an amazing variety of spices, temperings, and methods of cooking in which they can be savoured. Let me give you just one example. You can cook potatoes tempered with cumin with just a touch of turmeric to give them a pale golden tinge or you can start the cooking process by adding aromatic asafoetida to the hot oil and follow up with a perky mustard seed and ginger

flavouring. You can boil the potatoes and simmer them in a tomato gravy or you can deep fry them till they're soft-hearted but crunchy on the outside and serve them in a rich curd based curry. You can sprinkle pounded cardamom over· just before serving for a distinctive touch or then you can choose to highlight the flavour of poppy-seeds. Whichever way you decide to cook them, one fact is beyond doubt. Vegetables taste best if cooked with a minimum of fats and spices, that allow their own natural tastes to come through. Guard against overcooking, guilty of murdering nutrients and flavour. Experiment with different spices and seeds, team unusual vegetables together; combine pulses and greens. Be innovative and you will be well on the way to making the most of vegetables.

I must confess that it was difficult to decide which recipes to incorporate in this short section. I have tried to include all the vegetables and to highlight different regional specialities. You might be tempted to try out ladies' fingers cooked the way the Andhraites enjoy them, turnips the way they're savoured in the north in winter and a wholesome spinach, *Sai Bhaji*, which is a Sindhi speciality. There's a delicious fenugreek cooked with Maharashtrian overtones, brinjals in a rich Hyderabadi sauce and capsicum in an unusual preparation, teamed with gramflour. Cottage cheese features too, cooked in a creamy, tomato-based sauce. Finally, I couldn't resist adding sprouts, which, though not really a vegetable, just slipped into this section. There's yet another curry, a speciality of Rajasthan, which doesn't incorporate a green but still makes an interesting addition to any menu, specially if you have vegetarians to entertain. I hope the different flavours and colours will inspire you to be the only way you should when dealing with vegetables—creative.

ALU POSHTO

*Potatoes Cooked with Poppy Seeds.
This Bengali speciality is just such
an unusual way of enjoying both
poppy-seeds and potatoes.*

INGREDIENTS

5-6 tablespoons cooking oil
6 large potatoes, peeled and cubed
2 tablespoons poppy seeds, picked
2 green chillies, deseeded
2 dry red chillies
½ teaspoon turmeric powder
Salt to taste
¼ - ½ teaspoon sugar

UTENSILS

Any heavy-bottomed pan with a lid
An electric blender or grinder
A griddle

Method

1. Heat the oil to smoking point, then drop in the potatoes, in batches if necessary, and fry them all to a light brown. Remove from the oil and keep aside.

2. Heat the griddle and on it gently roast the poppy seeds till they're just beginning to change colour. Grind them along with the green chillies to as fine a paste as possible. You can do this in an electric grinder or manually on a grinding stone. In either case, you will need to add a few tablespoons of water.

3. In the same oil (you might need to add a little more) in which the potatoes were fried, add the red chillies, turmeric and salt and in a few seconds, the ground paste. Let the excess water evaporate and after the fat separates, fry for 4-5 minutes, stirring continuously.

4. Turn the lightly fried potatoes into the pan, stir to coat well with the mixture, add a little water, cover and leave on a slow fire to soften. This should take at least 15 minutes. The excess water should dry up too.

5. Add the sugar, stir well, and check seasoning before serving.

Serves 4.

Note: This recipe is medium hot. You can tone down or enhance the chillies if you like.

Rai Alu

*Potatoes Tempered with Mustard Seeds.
This is the way people in the south
prefer to cook potatoes—piquant, tempered with mustard seeds and fragrant
with curry leaves.*

INGREDIENTS
4 tablespoons cooking oil
1-2 whole, red chillies
1 teaspoon mustard seeds
2 small onions, chopped or sliced (optional)
1" piece of ginger, cubed finely
Green chillies to taste, sliced or chopped
1-1½ easpoons sambhar *powder*
*5 large potatoes, peeled and cubed in small
pieces*
Salt and pepper to taste
5-6 curry leaves, torn up
Juice of 1 lime

UTENSILS
A deep pan with a lid
A griddle

Method
1. Heat the oil. Drop in the dry red chillies.
Discard them when they darken.
2. Put in the mustard seeds. Cover the pan till
they stop spluttering.
3. Add the onions. Fry till softened, but don't let
them brown.

4. Add the ginger and chillies. Fry till the ginger
browns lightly.
5. Add the *sambhar* powder. Fry a second or
two.
6. Add the potatoes. Stir to coat well with the
mixture in the pan.
7. Add the rest of the ingredients except the lime
juice. Keep stirring the potatoes to ensure they
do not stick the bottom and start burning. After
about ten minutes, when they should have all
fried lightly, you can add half a cup of water,
cover the pan, put the griddle underneath and
continue the cooking till they're fully tenderised.
8. Just before serving, stir in the lime juice and
shake the pan gently to coat the potatoes evenly.

Serves 4.

*Note: If you're constrained for time, there is a
quicker way of making this. Boil the potatoes to
start with. Peel and cube them. Follow the
same method except for part of No. 7, which
describes the cooking process. Your boiled
potatoes will need just 5 minutes to simmer
with the tempering and spices.*

BHINDI ANDHRA SE

Ladies' Fingers Andhra style.
Cooked like this, this vegetable, also
called okra, has an unusual
flavour. The locals eat it very hot
but I have left that decision to you.

INGREDIENTS
2 tablespoons Bengal Gram
2 tablespoons White Gram
2 tablespoons fenugreek seeds
2 tablespoons cumin seeds
2 tablespoons coriander seeds
Red chilli powder to taste
4 tablespoons cooking oil
500 gms ladies fingers, washed, dried and
chopped
Salt to taste
³/₄-1 teaspoon mango powder (amchoor)

UTENSILS
A griddle
A deep pan with a lid
A plate

Method
1. Heat the griddle. You have to lightly roast the grams and the seeds on it. Do the grams first. Keep tossing and stirring them with a flat spoon till they change colour. Remove to the plate and do the seeds the same way. Grind all of them together with the red chilli powder. This amount of spices is more than you'll need for one recipe, so you can store it in an airtight bottle for future use.

2. Heat the oil in the deep pan. Drop the chopped lady's fingers into it. You need not cover the pan at this stage. Tossing occasionally, let the vegetable cook till it has lost all its stickiness. By this time it should be about half-cooked.
3. Add 4-5 teaspoons of the ground spices powder and salt. Stir to coat well.
4. Cover and cook till fully tenderised. You may like to put the griddle underneath.
5. A minute before taking off the fire, sprinkle over the mango powder. This imparts a delicious sourness. Taste and decide if you want to add a little more.

Serves 4.

Note: This same spices powder can be used to stuff whole ladies fingers. In that case, slit each one along one side, making sure you don't cut through to the other side. Push the spices powder into the slit and drop the vegetable into hot oil. Cover the pan, put the griddle underneath after about ten minutes of cooking time and continue the recipe on a slow fire. Stir occasionally. The whole process should take about 20-25 minutes.

GOBHI PANCHPHORAN

Cauliflower with Five Spices.
I tasted and got this recipe during my stay at an
erstwhile palace in Rajasthan. The cook, originally
a Nepali, developed his culinary skills under the
erstwhile Maharani. This dish had, the cook
admitted, a predominantly Bengali flavour. Try it.

INGREDIENTS

4-5 tablespoons oil
½ teaspoon cumin seeds
½ teaspoon fenugreek seeds
½ teaspoon mustard seeds
½ teaspoon aniseed
½ teaspoon nigella
1 large cauliflower, washed and cut in florets
Salt and red chilli powder to taste
½ teaspoon turmeric powder
5-6 cloves garlic, pounded roughly
1 teaspoon ground or sliced ginger
2 tablespoons fresh coriander, finely chopped

UTENSILS

An electric grinder or mortar and pestle
A deep pan with a lid

Method

1. Heat the oil in the deep pan.
2. Drop in all the seeds at once. Cover till they stop spluttering.
3. Add the cauliflower. Stir gently to coat with the tempered oil. Cook 5 minutes.
4. Add the salt, chilli and turmeric powder. Traditional Rajasthani cooking uses a generous amount of turmeric. (I have toned it down). Cover and cook till the vegetable is half done.
5. Add the garlic. Cover and cook till three-quarters done.
6. Add the ginger. Cover and cook till fully tenderised.
7. Garnish with the coriander before serving.

Serves 4.

SIMLA MIRCH BESAN KE SAATH

Capsicum with Gramflour.
An interesting way of enjoying this
piquant vegetable. You can add
roasted peanuts to it for added crunch
and nutrition.

INGREDIENTS
6 tablespoons cooking oil
A pinch of asafoetida
1 teaspoon mustard seeds
1 teaspoon cumin seeds
½ cup gramflour, sieved
½ teaspoon turmeric powder
Salt and chilli powder to taste
A few tablespoons water
500 gms capsicums,* washed, ribbed, deseeded
and chopped in bite-sized pieces
A handful of roasted peanuts (optional)

UTENSILS
A deep pan or heavy-bottomed pan with a lid
A griddle

Method
1. Heat the oil. Drop in the asafoetida. Let it change colour slightly.
2. Drop in the seeds. Cover till they stop spluttering.
3. Add the gramflour. Stir continuously till it browns and is aromatic.
4. Add the turmeric, salt and chilli. Fry another minute.

5. Add water enough to make a smooth, thickish paste.
6. Drop in the capsicum. Stir to coat well. Cover the pan, put the griddle underneath and cook till the capsicum is cooked, the water has all but evaporated, and the fat has separated. You need to stir occasionally during the cooking process (about 25-30 minutes) to avoid the flour sticking to the bottom and burning.
7. Sprinkle over the peanuts just before serving, if you're using them.

Serves 4.

* Perhaps you know this vegetable more commonly as bell-pepper.

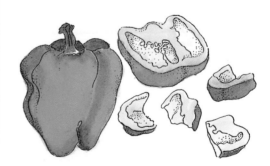

SHALGAM PUNJAB SE

Turnips from Punjab.
Soft, buttery, this recipe really
accentuates the natural flavour
of this vegetable. It's relatively
simple to cook, too.

INGREDIENTS

3-4 tablespoons cooking oil
Green chillies to taste, finely chopped
2 onions, finely chopped
2 small tomatoes, chopped
½ teaspoon turmeric powder
Salt to taste
½ teaspoon cumin powder
500 gms turnips, peeled, chopped and washed
1 cup water
1-2 teaspoons sugar
1½ tablespoons fresh coriander, finely chopped
White, unsalted butter

UTENSILS

A pressure cooker
A wooden masher

Method

1. Heat the oil. Don't make it too hot.
2. Drop in the chillies. Fry a few seconds.
3. Before the chillies start to darken, add the onions. Fry till just beginning to brown.

4. Add the tomatoes. Fry till the fat separates.
5. Add the turmeric, salt and cumin and fry a few more seconds.
6. Add the turnips. Stir to coat with the spices and oil.
7. Add the water and close the cooker. Allow it to reach maximum pressure then reduce heat and cook 15 minutes. Allow the pressure to reduce by itself. Open the cooker, add the sugar and mash the turnips to a puree. Dry out any excess water.
8. Mix in the coriander.
9. Serve with a generous dollop of white butter.

Serves 4.

Note: This is not quite the traditional way of making turnips. Normally, the turnips are pressure cooked with just salt, turmeric and chillies. Later they are mashed, sugared and tempered with browned onions and strips of ginger. The coriander garnish remains. They're equally delicious made this way.

PHALI NARIYAL KE SAATH

Beans with Coconut.
After that fairly rich turnip, a
delicately flavoured recipe, best
enjoyed when the beans are
fresh.

INGREDIENTS
1 tablespoon Bengal Gram
1 small coconut
4 tablespoons fresh coriander, chopped
4 cloves garlic, peeled and chopped
7-8 curry leaves, washed
Chillies to taste, chopped
3 tablespoons cooking oil
1 whole red chilli
1 teaspoon mustard seeds
500 gms beans, washed, tailed and cut into
pieces
Salt to taste
Juice of 1 lime

UTENSILS
Electric or manual grinder
A heavy bottomed pan with a lid
A griddle
A coconut scraper

Method
1. Heat the griddle. Lightly roast on it the gram.
Make sure it doesn't darken too much or it will
impart a bitter flavour. Keep aside.
2. Break the coconut. Grate the pulp. Make sure
the water doesn't go waste. Use it to grind
together the coconut pulp with the roasted gram,
the coriander, garlic, curry leaves and chillies.
You can do this in an electric or manual grinder
and add as much water as you need to make a
smooth paste.
3. In the pan, heat the oil. Drop in the red chilli.
Fry a few seconds.
4. Add the mustard seeds. Cover the pan
momentarily while they splutter.
5. Add the ground paste. Cook a few minutes.
6. Add the beans and salt. Stir to coat well with
the coconut mixture. Cover and cook on a
slow fire. You may need to put
the griddle underneath the
pan if you find the contents
sticking and burning after a
while. Continue to cook
till the beans are
tenderised and the excess
water has evaporated. This
should take 20-25 minutes.
7. Take off the fire and stir in
the lime juice, before serving.

Serves 4.

Note: We are talking here of the beans gene-
rally called french-beans in India. You could
however use any kind for equally good results.

SAI
BHAJI

Spinach Cooked in the Sindhi Style.
Traditionally eaten with rice, this is
truly a meal in itself incorporating
an iron-rich green, a dal *and all*
kinds of vegetables.

INGREDIENTS

4 tablespoons cooking oil
2 small onions, chopped
1½" piece of ginger, chopped
2 large tomatoes, chopped
½ teaspoon turmeric powder
Salt to taste
Green chillies to taste, chopped
2 cups mixed vegetables—brinjals, potatoes,
carrots, squash
A generous handful of Bengal Gram, soaked in
1 cup water
500 gms spinach, washed and chopped
3-4 tablespoons fresh soya, washed and
chopped

UTENSILS
A pressure cooker
A wooden spinach masher

Method

1. Heat the oil in the cooker. Fry the
onions lightly.

2. Add the ginger and fry a light brown.

3. Add the tomatoes, turmeric and salt. Fry till
the fat starts to separate.

4. Add all the rest of the ingredients. Stir well.
Close the cooker. Allow it to reach maximum
pressure, then reduce heat and cook 15 minutes.
Turn off the heat. Let the pressure reduce by
itself, then open cooker and with the wooden
masher, mash the vegetables and spinach
smooth. You should end up with a green puree
flecked with brown—the *dal.* As you mash, you
can put the pan on the fire in case there is any
excess water that needs to be dried up.

5. Check seasoning before serving.

Serves 4-6.

Note: There is another way of making this
spinach. Follow Step 1, then simply add all the
ingredients including the ginger and tomato
and cook together. Mash as described.

SARSON KA SAAG

Mustard Greens.
A unique North Indian speciality,
featuring three greens. Make it in
large quantities and freeze it for
another day or when it's no longer in
season.

INGREDIENTS

1 kg sarson *(mustard greens)*
250 gms bathua
250 gms spinach
50 gms ginger, chopped
50 gms garlic, chopped
1 large onion sliced
Green chillies to taste, chopped
Salt to taste
3-4 tablespoons cornmeal flour (makki ka atta)
3 tablespoons butter
1 teaspoon oil
1" piece of ginger, cut in strips
White unsalted butter

UTENSILS

A pressure cooker
A wooden spinach masher
A small pan to make the tempering

Method

1. Wash all the greens well in a number of changes of water. Chop.

2. Put all the greens into the cooker, along with the ginger, garlic, onion, green chillies, and salt. Close the cooker. After it reaches maximum pressure, reduce heat and keep half an hour.

3. Open the cooker. Mash the greens. While you're at it, add the cornmeal flour and keep stirring till the greens are a smooth, thick puree. Dry out any excess water.

4. Heat the butter and oil in a separate pan. Add the ginger. Fry light brown. Turn into the greens and stir well.

5. Top with a generous dollop of white butter before serving.

6. Traditionally, brown sugar is served with this. You can try it and see if you like the mingling of salty and sweet flavours.

Serves 8.

Note: Bathua *is another variety of spinach, usually available in winter at the same time as* sarson. *Use it if you can get it otherwise make the* Saag *even without it, increasing the quantity of spinach.*

85

KARELA CHANNE KI DAL KE SAATH

Bitter Gourds with Bengal Gram.
One of my favourite recipes.
Apart from being a delicious
mingling of flavours, it's whole-
some too.

INGREDIENTS

500 gms bitter gourds, washed and scraped
3 tablespoons Bengal Gram, washed and
soaked
5 tablespoons cooking oil
1 teaspoon cumin seeds
4 onions, sliced fine
6 cloves garlic
1" piece of ginger, ground with the garlic
1-2 green chillies, chopped
1/2 teaspoon turmeric powder
3 tablespoons tomato puree or 3 tomatoes,
pureed
Salt to taste

UTENSILS

A heavy-bottomed pan with a lid
A small pan with a lid to cook the dal
A griddle

Method

1. Cut the gourds into slices and deseed them. Sprinkle salt all over and keep aside for at least half an hour (preferably for a couple of hours), then wash well in a number of changes of water. Squeeze before keeping aside. This is to diminish its natural bitterness.

2. Separately, half-cook the soaked *dal*—it should get soft but not broken. Don't throw away the water in which you boil it.

3. Heat the oil. Lightly fry the gourds. Remove from the oil and keep aside.

4. Into the same oil, drop the cumin seeds. Don't allow them to darken too much.

5. Add the onions. Fry to a light brown.

6. Add the ginger and garlic. Fry to a golden brown.

7. Add the chillies, turmeric, salt and tomatoes. Fry till the fat separates, adding a few teaspoons of water if needed.

8. Add the gourds and *dal* to the mixture in the pan, stirring to coat it well. Add about 1/2 cup of the reserved water. Cover the pan, put the griddle underneath and cook till the gourds and the gram are fully tenderised and the fat has separated.

Serves 4.

METHI
ALU

*Fenugreek with Potatoes.
I always made this combination
with just a tempering of cumin
seeds, adding salt and turmeric
as the dish cooked. A friend from
Bombay insisted I try her
variation. I did. It's delicious.*

INGREDIENTS

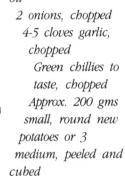

4 tablespoons cooking
oil
2 onions, chopped
4-5 cloves garlic,
chopped
Green chillies to
taste, chopped
Approx. 200 gms
small, round new
potatoes or 3
medium, peeled and
cubed
500 gms fresh fenugreek,
washed, chopped, salted and left to drain
Salt to taste

UTENSILS
A heavy-bottomed pan with a lid

A griddle

Method
1. Heat the oil. Put in the onions. Fry lightly.
2. Add the garlic. Stir and fry a few minutes more.
3. Add the green chillies and the potatoes. Fry till the potatoes are lightly browned.
4. Add the fenugreek and salt. Stir, cover the pan and cook on a slow fire for about 10 minutes. During this time, the fenugreek will exude water. As it begins to get dry, put the griddle underneath the pan and continue to cook till it is fully cooked and the potatoes are tender. You have to stir occasionally during the cooking process, which takes a total of about half an hour.

Serves 4.

BAGARA BAINGAN

Hyderabadi Brinjals.
A very tempting Eid speciality. Tradi-
tionally, it is very strong on chillies
and I have repeatedly been told that
that is the only way it should be. You
might like to tone it down, however, if
you prefer.

INGREDIENTS

500 gms small, round brinjals
Oil for frying
4 onions
3 tablespoons tamarind, soaked in 3 cups
water
1/2 fresh coconut, grated
2 tablespoons peanuts, lightly roasted
2 tablespoons sesame seeds, (til), *lightly roasted*
2 tablespoons poppy seeds (khus khus), *lightly roasted*
2 teaspoons cumin powder
2 teaspoons fenugreek seeds, ground
2 tablespoons red chilli or to taste
Green chillies to taste, chopped (optional)
1 teaspoon turmeric powder
5 tomatoes, pureed
Salt to taste
Tamarind, the size of 2 small lemons, soaked
in 3/4 cup water
8-9 curry leaves

UTENSILS

A large heavy-bottomed pan or karhai *(wok)*
An electric or manual grinder
A slotted spoon
A coconut scraper
A bowl for the tamarind

Method

1. Cut a cross in the tip of each brinjal, running three quarters of the way up. Don't remove the stem or let the brinjal disintegrate. Sprinkle salt all over and leave to drain for half an hour.

2. Put the oil on to heat. You have to deep fry so you will need at least half a panful. When the oil is medium hot, pat each brinjal dry and slip into the oil. Increase the heat for about 5 minutes then reduce it again and continue to cook till the brinjals are cooked through. They will look wrinkled and a slightly different shade of purple than what you started out with. Drain from the oil and keep aside. Keep only about 4 tablespoons of oil in the pan. Remove the excess.

3. While the brinjals are frying, you can roast the onions. Put them directly on the flame and let them get charred on all sides. Slip off the skins, wash the onions, remove any charred bits that are still clinging and grind the onions along with the coconut, the peanuts, sesame seeds, poppy seeds.

4. To the ground paste, add the cumin, fenugreek, chillies, both red and green, turmeric, tomatoes, and salt. Mix to a thick paste with the strained tamarind water and pulp.

5. Reheat the oil in which the brinjals were fried. Pour in the tamarind-coconut paste. Cook on a slow fire till the oil starts to separate. This will take at least half an hour.

6. Slip in the brinjals and curry leaves. Simmer 10 minutes before taking off the fire.

Serves 6-8.

Note: This recipe improves with keeping. Since it is laborious, you might in any case prefer to make it a day ahead, specially if you're entertaining.

Perhaps you are more familiar with this vegetable being called egg-plant or aubergine. For this recipe I have used the small, purple variety.

Matki Moongphali ke Saath

Nutty sprouts.
A nutritious combination, this is the way
sprouts, called matki, *are enjoyed all over*
Gujarat and Maharashtra.

INGREDIENTS

1 cup Whole Green Gram
3 tablespoons cooking oil
½ teaspoon mustard seeds
½ teaspoon White Gram
2 whole red chillies
2 small onions, finely chopped
1" piece of ginger, finely cubed
Green chillies to taste, finely chopped
Salt to taste
1-2 teaspoons sugar
Juice of 1 lime
2-3 tablespoons roasted peanuts

UTENSILS

A bowl for sprouting the gram
A heavy bottomed pan with a lid
A cloth

Method

1. Sprout the gram. To do this, soak it in water for 8-10 hours then throw away the water, cover the gram with a wet cloth and leave it for another 8-10 hours in a warm, dry place. At the end of this time, you will find that the gram has sprouted and is crunchy to taste.

2. Heat the oil. Add the mustard seeds, gram and red chillies. The seeds will splutter and the chillies will turn dark. You may discard the latter if you like.

3. Add the onions and ginger and fry till the onions are light brown.

4. Add the chillies, salt, sugar. Stir well and fry a few seconds.

5. Add the sprouts, stir well, add ¼-½ cup of water, cover the pan and cook on low heat till the sprouts are as tender as you would like them. This will take 10-20 minutes, depending on how soft or crunchy you prefer them.

6. Stir in the lime juice and peanuts just before serving. Also just before you eat, check seasonings and add more lime juice or sugar if needed.

Serves 4.

MAZEDAR
TORI

Flavourful Zucchini.
Simple, succulent, flavoured
with dill, this is a delightful
recipe.

INGREDIENTS

3 tablespoons cooking oil
1 teaspoon cumin seeds
2 onions, finely chopped
Green chillies to taste, chopped and deseeded
A pinch of turmeric powder
½ tablespoon fresh, chopped or 1 teaspoon dried
dill (soya)
2 small tomatoes, chopped
700 gms zucchini, peeled and cut in rings
Salt to taste
½ teaspoon sugar
1 tablespoon fresh coriander leaves, chopped

UTENSILS

A heavy bottomed pan with a lid

Method

1. Heat the oil. Drop in the cumin seeds. Let them turn a shade darker.
2. Add the onions and fry till softened but not browned.
3. Add the green chillies and turmeric and fry a few seconds more.
4. Add the dill and tomatoes and cook till the fat separates.
5. Add the vegetable and the salt. Stir well, cover and let it cook 7-10 minutes.
6. Add the sugar and cook another few minutes or till the vegetable is fully tenderised and the fat has separated. Take off the fire.
7. Serve garnished with the coriander.

Serves 4.

Note: I have not mentioned the addition of water during the cooking process. Normally, if the zucchini is in season and very fresh, it may not be necessary but this does depend on the quality of the vegetable so do check on it while it's cooking. If it does not have enough of its own juices, add a little water to help it cook. Also, in case you are in a hurry and wish to pressure cook, it takes just a minute or two after the cooker reaches maximum pressure.

Bottle gourd (lauki) *can also be cooked this way.*

SOOKHA MATAR PANEER

Peas with Cottage Cheese.
A minimum of spices makes this
a wonderfully simple yet
flavourful way of enjoying both
peas and cottage cheese.

INGREDIENTS
250 gms cottage cheese
3 tablespoons cooking oil
2 onions, finely chopped
Green chillies to taste, finely chopped
2 small tomatoes, finely chopped (optional)
½ teaspoon cumin powder
½ teaspoon turmeric powder
Salt and pepper to taste
2¼ cups peas, parboiled
1 tablespoon lime juice
2 tablespoons fresh coriander, washed and finely chopped
1 teaspoon garam masala *(optional)*

UTENSILS
A pan with a lid

Method

1. Crumble the cottage cheese by hand to the consistency of coarse breadcrumbs. Keep aside.
2. In the pan, heat the oil and add the onions. Fry on gentle heat till softened but not browned.
3. Add the chilli, tomatoes (if you're using them) as well as the cumin, turmeric, salt and pepper. Fry gently till the tomatoes get cooked and the fat floats to the top.
4. Add the peas and fry a minute or two.
5. Add the cheese. Cover and cook till the excess water from the cheese evaporates and the peas are fully tenderised.
6. Remove from the fire and stir in the lemon juice and coriander.
7. Garnish with the *garam masala*, if you're using it, before serving.

Serves 4.

Note: You can omit the cottage cheese from this recipe if you like and cook the peas by themselves. Of course, you will need a larger quantity and you might have to add a little water to help them tenderise.

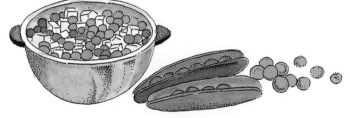

SHAHI PANEER

*Cottage Cheese in a Creamy Tomato Curry.
Doesn't this sound thoroughly diet-wrecking
and delectable? It's both.*

INGREDIENTS
3 tablespoons cooking oil
1 onion, finely chopped
½" piece of ginger, grated or ground
Green chillies to taste, deseeded and sliced
A pinch of turmeric
2 tablespoons fresh coriander, chopped
2 large tomatoes, pureed or blanched and chopped
1 tablespoon tomato sauce
Salt to taste
½ teaspoon black pepper
1 cup cream, lightly beaten
400 gms cottage cheese, cubed
½ teaspoon garam masala

UTENSILS
A heavy bottomed pan
A plate

Method
1. Heat the oil. Add the onions. Fry till softened but not browned.
2. Add the ginger and chillies, and fry a few minutes, stirring and adding a few teaspoons of water if needed.
3. Add the turmeric, coriander and tomatoes and fry till the fat separates.
4. Add the sauce, salt, and pepper and keep on the fire another few seconds.
5. Just before serving, add the cream. Heat through gently but do not boil the mixture or the *ghee* will separate. Add the cottage cheese. It would be better if you left it to drain for about half an hour before adding it to the sauce. The best way to do this is to put it on a slightly tilted plate. If you prefer, you may fry the cheese lightly before adding it to the sauce, though I don't normally like to do it.
6. Serve garnished with the *garam masala*.

Serves 4.

LAUKI KOFTA CURRY

Bottle Gourd Balls in Curry.
Succulent koftas *that need some*
practice to perfect but are really a delightful
addition to any meal, once you've
got the hang of it.

INGREDIENTS
1 bottle gourd, weighing about 700 gms
Salt to taste
1-2 finely chopped green chillies
$\frac{1}{2}$-1 teaspoon dried fenugreek leaves
1 teaspoon ginger, ground
8-10 tablespoons gramflour
A small ball of tamarind, washed, deseeded
and cut into 20-22 tiny pieces
1 cup oil

UTENSILS
A deep pan
A vegetable grater
Brown paper
Another heavy-bottomed pan

Method
1. Peel and grate the bottle gourd. Squeeze out all the water by pressing hard between the palms.
2. Mix in the salt, chillies, fenugreek and ginger. Mix together evenly.
3. Start adding the gramflour by tablespoonfuls. Keep sprinkling all over and mixing into the bottle gourd with your hand, till the mixture becomes a little thicker than dropping consistency. The secret of soft *koftas* is the amount of gramflour you add; too little and the *koftas* might break; too much and they will be hard and the flavour of the vegetable will be smothered. After a couple of trials, however, you should be able to master it.
4. While you're mixing the flour in, put the oil on to heat. Let it reach smoking point then reduce heat and let it remain on the fire.
5. As soon as the mixture is ready, take a little into your hand, roll it into a ball, press a tiny piece of tamarind into the middle, reshape and drop into the oil. Fry on medium heat to a golden brown. Drain on the brown paper.
6. To make the curry, use the recipe for Fritters in a Curry (see section on Pulses) or for that matter, the Creamy Tomato curry (see the last recipe).
7. Just before you're ready to serve, heat through the curry, drop in the fried *koftas* and simmer for 7–10 minutes.

Serves 4–6.
Note: This is an excellent way of disguising bottle-gourd, or squash as it is also called, for those who otherwise shun this delicate vegetable!

GATTA SAMODE KA

Gramflour Slices in Curry.
A Rajasthani speciality that
will grace any table.

INGREDIENTS
For the gatta
500 gms gramflour
Red chilli powder to taste
1 teaspoon turmeric powder
3 teaspoons aniseed
Salt to taste
2 teaspoons baking soda
2 teaspoons oil
Water
For the curry
5 tablespoons cooking oil
5 onions, finely chopped
1 teaspoon whole black pepper
A few sticks of cinnamon
3 green cardamoms
250 gms curds, lightly beaten
Salt to taste
A pinch of turmeric powder
Red chilli powder to taste
1 teaspoon coriander powder

UTENSILS
A large pan to simmer the gatta
Another to make the gravy

Method
1. Bind together all the ingredients for the *gatta*. Use just as much water as you need to make a stiff but pliable dough.
2. Shape into 4 sausage–shaped rolls.
3. In a large pan (in which the rolls can fit) bring some water to boil. It should be enough to immerse the rolls. Once the water comes to the boil, drop the rolls in, cover the pan and steam the rolls for about 20 minutes.
4. Take the rolls out of the water and cut into thickish circles. Don't throw away the water in which they steamed.
5. To make the curry, heat the oil in the other pan . Fry the onions a golden brown.
6. Drop in the pepper, cinnamon, and carda-moms. Fry a few seconds more.
7. Add the curds and the rest of the ingredients. Stir and cook till the fat starts to separate.
8. Add some of the reserved water to make the curry the consistency you desire.
9. Slip in the *gatta* and simmer 5 minutes. Add a little more water to thin the curry if you like. It should in any case be a thickish one.

Serves 8–10.

Doodh Wala Bhutta

Milky Corn Curry.
The flavours of Gujarat—corn simmered in
a delicately flavoured, white curry. It must
rank as one of the best ways of savouring
this vegetable.

INGREDIENTS

4 fresh, soft corn cobs
2 tablespoons fresh, grated coconut
4 tablespoons fresh coriander, chopped
Green chillies to taste, chopped
1" piece of ginger, chopped
3 tablespoons cooking oil
1 teaspoon mustard seeds
7–8 curry leaves, torn up
Salt to taste
½ cup milk
Some fresh coriander, finely chopped

UTENSILS

A pressure cooker
Another pan
An electric or manual grinder

Method

1. Put the corn into the pressure cooker with a few cups of water. Allow the cooker to reach maximum pressure, then reduce heat and keep on the fire for 10–20 minutes. This depends on how hard or soft the ears are to start with. If you have time, allow the pressure to reduce by itself.

Open the cooker and cut each corn cob into about 4 pieces each. Keep aside. Don't throw away the water in which the corn was boiled.
2. Grind to a thick paste the coconut, coriander, chillies and ginger. You can use some of the water in which the corn was boiled if you need.
3. Rub the ground paste into the corn and let it marinate for at least half an hour.
4. In the second pan, heat the oil. Drop in the mustard seeds. Let them splutter.
5. Add to the pan the corn along with some of the water in which it was boiled and the curry leaves and salt. It should make a thickish gravy. Cover the pan and simmer about 10 minutes.
6. Just before serving, heat the milk and add it to the pan. Stir to blend well and serve immediately.
7. Garnish with the fresh coriander.

Serves 4.

Note: This curry is normally made this way, i.e., with the corn cobs cut in pieces. If you prefer, however, you can modify it a little by removing the kernels from the ears.

RAI
SABZI

Vegetables Tempered with Mustard Seeds.
A most satisfying curry incorporating as
many—or as few—vegetables as you
fancy. Thickened with wheat–flour and
tempered with mustard seeds, it has a
most distinctive flavour.

INGREDIENTS

3 tablespoons cooking oil; 1½ "piece of ginger
chopped fine; 2 green chillies, sliced or
chopped; ½ teaspoon turmeric powder;
1 teaspoon coriander powder; 2 tomatoes,
chopped; 2–3 potatoes, peeled and cubed;
10 cloves garlic, peeled but left whole; 2 tindas,
peeled and cut in halves; 2–3 long brinjals, cut
in thick rings; 7–8 whole ladies' fingers; 6–8
cubes bottle gourd or zucchini; 4 small whole
onions (optional); a few waris (dumplings
made of pounded pulses and spices) (optional)
salt to taste; 3 tablespoons wholewheat flour
(atta); A few tablespoons water; 1 tablespoon
oil; 1 teaspoon mustard seeds; 1 tablespoon
fresh coriander, finely chopped

UTENSILS

A karhai or any other heavy–bottomed pan
with a lid
A small pan for the tempering.

Method

1. Heat the oil and add the ginger and chillies.
Stirring continuously, allow them to
brown lightly.

2. Add the turmeric and coriander powder and
fry a few seconds.

3. Add the tomatoes and fry till the fat separates.

4. Add the potatoes, garlic and a little water.
Cover and let the potatoes cook for about 5–7
minutes then add the rest of the quicker
cooking vegetables, and the *waris*, if you're
using them. Add salt and 2 ½ cups water. Cover
and simmer till all the vegetables are almost done.
If at all you stir during the cooking time, do it
gently so the vegetables don't start to disintegrate.

5. Mix the flour to a smooth paste with the water.
Add it to the vegetables. Stir continuously but
gently to prevent the flour from sticking to the
bottom. Check the consistency of the curry. If it is
too thick, add a little water. Boil for a few
minutes then remove from the fire.

6. If you are not serving immediately, take off the
fire at this stage but when you're ready   to eat,
bring the curry to the boil
again. Heat the oil in the
small pan and drop in the
mustard seeds. As soon as
they stop spluttering, turn
into the curry. Stir briefly,
and serve garnished with
the coriander.

Serves 4-5.

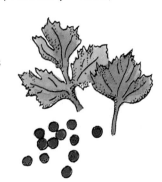

SAVOURING THE MEATS

MEATS

If you read between the lines of some of these recipes, you will discover that they have interesting stories to tell. They talk of their past, of their Mughlai and Persian and Portugese influences. They tell of their present too, of the climate, culture and local influences that make them what they are. Read about saffron and you can make a fairly safe guess that the recipe hails from Kashmir, the land where this exotic plant grows and finds it's way not only into the cooking but also the local tea, the *kahwa*. When the delicate tasting coconut asserts itself to flavour the cuisine, you know you are in the coastal regions, in the land where the palm–trees grow, and where every kitchen is familiar with their brown–husked, milky–interiored fruit. Talk of hot, sea–food, of Vindaloo curries and you can imagine yourself amongst the lively people of Goa with their Portugese past and their boisterous love of music, wine, dance and good, fiery food. Savour that exquisite blend of the sweet with the sour and you could well be trying out a Gujarati recipe or for that matter, a Parsi one just as that rich, robust–sounding Butter Chicken could only be a creation of the equally robust people of

Punjab. The *Shikampuri Kabab* and *Pasanday* take you back to the era of sumptuous royal feasts and banquets, while two recipes for fish— one accentuating mustard, the other a delicate combination of curds and spices—testify to the age–old Bengali expertise with sea–food. Here they all are for you, these diverse flavours, with their own stories to tell. As in the last sections, I have tried to make them as varied as possible. I hope you will enjoy your travels with them.

In many of the recipes, particularly those using meat, you will notice that in the first steps, the meat may be browned in hot oil to which whole spices (cloves, cardamom, cinnamon) have been added. Alternately, the meat could be fried in a paste of browned onions, ginger and garlic. As the juices from the meat are released and evaporate, you will find it and the spices sticking to the bottom. Add a few teaspoons of water or curds at regular intervals to scrape them off and avoid them burning. This is perhaps the most laborious part of meat cookery but one which gives an unsubstitutable flavour because the meat imbibes the accentuated, roasted flavour of the spices during the process of frying in the

hot oil. Alternately, of course, the meat could be marinated for a number of hours or even overnight in a mixture of curds, spices, garlic and ginger. This is yet another way of allowing the meat to absorb the various flavours. After the marination, the meat is normally cooked on a slow fire or as in the case of the Creamy Boneless Chicken and the *Tandoori* Fish, in an oven. The Rich Meat Curry is also a good example of this type of cooking. You will also perhaps notice two very different methods of cooking at work in the two Kashmiri recipes I have selected. In the first, the *Kashmiri Gosht*, the meat is fried, as I described earlier, then tenderised and garnished with nuts and cream. In the second recipe, on the other hand, the meat is boiled with all the spices and curds and the stock is then thickened with browned onions to make a rich gravy.

Because of the first steps in meat cookery described earlier i.e. frying and browning in oil, you will use more oil than is good for health and when your dish is done, you will find it floating on top. If this distresses you, just skim it off and keep it to use in some other preparation.

The meat most commonly used in India is mutton or lamb. You can substitute it with beef if you prefer. Similarly, the varieties of fish available here can be interchanged with kinds more easily available wherever you happen to be living. I must mention also, that specially in the case of meat cookery, I use a pressure cooker. You can, if you like, cook in any heavy–bottomed pan preferably with a well–fitting lid though of course, you can cater to a little more than doubling of cooking times.

ROGAN JOSH

Curried Lamb.
This meat, aromatic with spices, has a rich brown
colour because of the caramelised sugar and is a good
example of the frying process described in the
introduction to the section. It is best served with naans,
parathas or rice.

INGREDIENTS

6 tablespoons cooking oil
A large pinch of asafoetida
2-3 black cardamoms, pounded
1 teaspoon whole black pepper
2 tablespoons sugar
1 kg meat, washed
2" piece of ginger, chopped fine or ground
2 cups curds, lightly beaten
2 large tomatoes, chopped
Red chilli powder to taste

1 teaspoon coriander powder
Salt to taste
1 ½ cups of water
1-1½ tablespoons butter (optional)
1 tablespoon fresh coriander, finely chopped

UTENSILS

A pressure cooker

Method

1. Heat the oil. Drop in the asafoetida. Allow it to darken and stop fizzing.

2. Add the whole spices. Fry a minute till they are aromatic.

3. Add the sugar. Stir occasionally till it caramel izes. It should turn golden brown.

4. Add the meat. Fry till the meat juices evaporate.

5. Add the ginger. Fry till lightly browned.

6. Add the curds, tomatoes, chilli, coriander and salt. Cook till all the curds are absorbed. You have to keep stirring frequently.

7. Add the water. Close the cooker. Allow it to come to maximum pressure, then reduce heat and keep 25-35 minutes, till the meat is well tenderised, and the gravy is the consistency you desire.

8. Stir in the butter if you're using it and serve garnished with the fresh coriander.
Serves 6.

KASHMIRI GOSHT

*Meat Cooked with Nuts.
1 picked up this recipe from a
Kashmiri cook. Rich in taste and
looks, this aromatic dish uses nuts
and curds to effect, and is a good
example of cooking that can be
simple yet so effective.*

INGREDIENTS

6 tablespooons cooking oil

3 onions, sliced thin

5 small sticks of cinnamon

5-6 cloves

5 large black cardamoms, pounded

1 kg meat, washed

1 tablespoon almonds, blanched and sliced

1 tablespoon cashewnuts, sliced lengthwise

1 tablespoon raisins

3 tablespoon cream or top-of-the milk, lightly beaten

1— 1 $\frac{1}{2}$ cups curds, lightly beaten

1 tablespoon fresh coriander, finely chopped

Fresh green chillies to taste, chopped

UTENSILS

A pressure cooker

Method

1. Heat the oil. Add the onions. Fry light brown.

2. Add the whole spices. Fry another few minutes.

3. Add the meat. Fry till a rich brown.

4. Add 1$\frac{1}{2}$ cups water. Close the cooker and allow it to reach maximum pressure, then reduce heat and keep 25-35 minutes. Open cooker and check that the meat has tenderised and the liquids have all but evaporated. If you are not ready to serve yet, keep the meat aside for the moment. When you are ready to eat, heat it through and add to it the rest of the ingredients except the last two, which you can use to garnish the dish.

Serves 6.

Note: The amount of curds used in the recipe is variable. 1 cup will give you a thick, clinging gravy, 1$\frac{1}{2}$ cups a slightly thinner one.

TABAK MANS

Meat Cooked in the Kashmiri style.
Though another preparation from the
northern region, see how differently this
speciality is cooked.

INGREDIENTS

1 kg meat, washed
2 cups curds, lightly beaten
1 cup water
2 small pieces cinnamon
5 cloves
3 teaspoons ground ginger
3 teaspoons ground garlic
Whole red or green chillies to taste
2 teaspoons cumin seeds
2-3 bay leaves
2 onions, ground
Salt to taste
5 tablespoons cooking oil
2 onions, ground
Green chillies to taste, chopped or ground with
the onions
A pinch of saffron
1 tablespoon coriander, chopped

UTENSILS

A pressure cooker
Another heavy-bottomed pan with a lid
A strainer or muslin cloth

Method

1. Put into the pressure cooker the first twelve ingredients. Close the cooker, and after it comes to maximum pressure, reduce heat and keep 15 minutes. Open the cooker—the meat should be about half cooked.

2. Remove the pieces of meat from the gravy. Keep aside.

3. Strain the gravy through fine muslin or a strainer. Press down with a spoon to extract all the flavour.

4. Heat the oil. Add the onions. Fry to a golden brown.

5. To the pan on the fire, add the meat and after 5 minutes, the strained liquid and the green chillies. Bring to the boil, then reduce heat, cover and cook on a slow fire till the meat is completely tenderised, the gravy has thickened, and the oil separated. Check the seasoning.

6. Sprinkle over the saffron and garnish with the coriander.

Serves 6.

NARIYAL GOSHT

Meat Curry with Coconut.
Curds, coconut, lots of coriander and no onions or spices go into
making this recipe special indeed. When you're thumbing
through your recipes, looking for something different, try this.
Cook chicken too this way — you will be delighted

INGREDIENTS

1 cup curds, lightly beaten; A pinch of saffron;
1 kg meat, washed; 6 tablespoons cooking oil
A small piece of cinnamon; 5 cloves; 5 green
cardamoms, pounded; 4 onions, ground;
2" piece of ginger, ground; 10-12 cloves garlic,
ground; 2 tablespoons mint ground with
6 tablespoons fresh coriander and green chillies
to taste; Salt to taste; 1 large coconut, grated; 2
cups water, heated; 20 almonds, ground to a
paste with water or curds; 1½ -2 tablespoons
poppy seeds, lightly roasted and ground;
1½ tablespoons fresh coriander

UTENSILS

A pressure cooker
2 small bowls for the coconut milk
An electric or manual grinder

A muslin cloth

Method

1. Add the saffron to the curds and pour over the meat. Keep aside to marinate for at least half an hour.

2. Meanwhile, heat the oil. Add the whole spices. Fry for a minute.

3. Add the onions. Fry light bown.

4. Add the ginger and garlic. Fry golden brown.

5. Add the mint, coriander, chillies and salt and fry till the fat starts to separate.

6. Lift out the pieces of meat from the curds and put in to the pan on the fire. Fry till lightly browned.

7. While the meat is frying, pour 1 cup of water over the grated coconut. Squeeze through a muslin cloth to extract the milk. Keep this aside. It is the first milk. Repeat the process with the remaining water. This is the second milk.

8. After the meat has fried, add to the pan the curds in which the meat was marinated and the second milk. Close the cooker, allow it to reach maximum pressure, then reduce heat and keep on the fire 25-35 minutes or till the meat is well tenderised. Open the cooker and add the first coconut milk, almonds and poppy seeds. You can, if you prefer, mix the three together to a smooth paste before adding them. Simmer till the curry is the consistency you desire.

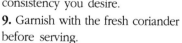

9. Garnish with the fresh coriander before serving.

Serves 6.

PALAK GOSHT

Meat cooked with Spinach.
After that elegant, delicate tasting curry, a more
dominating one. This time, the meat is cooked in
spinach, a blending of flavours reminiscent of
north Indian winters.

INGREDIENTS
6 tablespoons cooking oil
3 cloves
1" stick of cinnamon
2 black cardamoms, pounded
4 onions, finely chopped or grated
2" piece of ginger
1 pod garlic, ground with the ginger
Green chillies to taste, chopped
4 largeish tomatoes, chopped or pureed
$\frac{1}{2}$ teaspoon turmeric powder
2 teaspoons coriander powder
Salt to taste
500 gms meat, washed
500 gms spinach, ground
2 teaspoons cream (optional)

UTENSILS
A pressure cooker or deep pan
An electric or manual grinder

Method
1. Heat the oil. Add the cloves, cinnamon and cardamoms. Fry a minute.
2. Add the onions. Fry light brown.
3. Add the ginger-garlic paste and fry golden brown. Add a few teaspoons of water during this cooking if needed.
4. Add the chillies and tomatoes and fry till the fat separates.
5. Add the turmeric, coriander and salt and fry a few seconds more.
6. Add the meat and fry till lightly browned on all sides.
7. Add the spinach, stir well, add $\frac{1}{2}$ cup water and close the cooker. Allow it to reach maximum pressure, then reduce heat and keep on the fire about 20-30 minutes or till the meat is tenderised and the spinach is clinging to the meat. Boil away any excess liquid if needed. If you prefer not to pressure cook, cook covered on a slow fire—it should take about an hour, and you will probably need to add more water.
8. Serve garnished with a swirl of cream.

Serves 6.

SHAHI GOSHT

Rich Meat Curry.
Simple yet special, this meat is
marinated in curds, then cooked and
finished with cashewnuts and cream.

INGREDIENTS

1 cup fresh curds
1½ teaspoons coriander powder
Salt to taste
500 gms meat, washe
4 tablespoons cooking oil
2 black cardamoms, pounde
3 green cardamoms, pounded
1 teaspoon cumin seeds
3 onions, finely sliced
2" piece of ginger, ground or grated
Green chillies, to taste, chopped
25 cashews, ground to a fine paste
3 tablespoons cream or top of the milk
Juice of half a lime

UTENSILS

A pan to marinate the meat
A pressure cooker
An electric blender or manual grinder to grind
the cashews

Method

1. Lightly beat the curds and mix into it the
coriander and salt. Rub this mixture well into the
meat, pour the excess over and keep aside for
an hour at least and longer if possible.

2. Heat the oil. Drop in the cardamoms and after
a few seconds, the cumin. Let the cumin turn a
few shades darker.

3. Add the onions and fry golden brown. This is
best done on medium heat.

4. Add the ginger and chillies and fry
for a minute.

5. Add the meat along with all the marinade.
Add ½ cup of water. Close the cooker and allow
it to come to maximum pressure. Lower the heat
and keep on the fire 20-25 minutes.
Open the cooker. The
meat should be tenderised
and the curry thickish. If
it is too thin, boil
away some of the
excess liquid.

6. Blend the cashews
with the cream and stir
into the meat. Cover and
cook another 10 minutes.

7. Before serving, stir in the
lime juice.

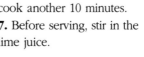

Serves 4.

114

PASANDAY

*Special cuts of flattened, boneless
meat, these* Pasanday *from
Lucknow are a treat.*

INGREDIENTS

6 tablespoons cooking oil
2 small sticks of cinnamon
5 cloves
2 black cardamoms, pounded
4 onions, grated or ground
1 tablespoon ground ginger
1 tablespoon ground garlic
*2-3 tablespoons fresh coriander, ground with
the ginger and garlic*
Green chillies to taste, also ground or chopped
*4 tablespoons poppy seeds, ground to a paste
with water*
1 teaspoon cumin powder
1 teaspoon coriander powder
Red chilli and salt to taste
1 kg Pasanday meat
*3 tablespoons cashew nuts, ground in milk to a
paste*
$^1/_2$ cup cream, lightly beaten
Green chillies, sliced

UTENSILS
A heavy-bottomed pan with a lid

Method

1. Heat the oil. Drop in the whole spices.
Fry a minute.

2. Add the onions. Fry pinkish.

3. Add the ginger, garlic, coriander and chillies.
Fry another 5-7 minutes, adding a few teaspoons
water, if needed.

4. Add the poppy seeds. Fry another few
minutes, stirring constantly.

5. Add the cumin, coriander, salt and chilli. Fry a
few seconds. Add the meat. Brown lightly.

6. Add 2 cups hot water.
Cover the pan and
cook on a slow
fire till tender.

7. Just before
serving, add the
cashews and the
cream. Heat through
gently, without
boiling.

8. Serve garnished with the
green chillies.

Serves 6.

CHOPS DO-PIAZA

*Chops with Plenty of Onions.
These chops, cooked with plenty
of onions and piquant with
vinegar are mouth-watering.*

INGREDIENTS

6 tablespoons cooking oil
1 teaspoon cumin
Green chillies to taste, chopped

2 teaspoons sugar
8 onions, thinly sliced in rings
2¹/₂" piece of ginger, ground
9-10 cloves garlic, ground
1 kg chops, well washed
Salt to taste
1 teaspoon black pepper
2-3 tablespoons white vinegar

UTENSILS

A pressure cooker.

Method

1. Heat the oil. Add the cumin and green chillies and fry for a few seconds.

2. Add the sugar, and after a few seconds, half the onions. Fry light brown.

3. Add the ginger-garlic paste and fry till golden brown.

4. Add the chops and on a slow fire, brown gently on all sides.

5. Add the salt, pepper and vinegar. Adjust seasoning so that the result tastes neither oversweet nor sour.

6. Add 1 cup hot water, stir well, close the cooker and let it come to maximum pressure then reduce heat and keep on the fire 15 minutes.

7. After you open the cooker, check that the chops are tender and add the remaining onion rings. Simmer 5-7 minutes more and serve immediately.

Serves 6.

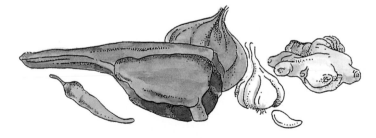

Keemo Tatrelo

Sweet and Sour Minced Meat.
This is the way the Parsis
savour minced meat. It's an easy
recipe too with an interesting
addition—vinegar and sugar—that
gives it a distinctive taste.

INGREDIENTS

6 tablespoons cooking oil
4 onions, chopped
5-6 curry leaves, torn up
Green chillies to taste, chopped
2" piece of ginger, ground
10-12 cloves garlic, ground
2 teaspoons cumin seeds, roasted and ground
$\frac{1}{2}$ teaspoon turmeric powder
1 teaspoon black pepper
Salt to taste
1 kg mince, washed
4 tomatoes, blanched and chopped
2 teaspoons vinegar
2-3 teaspoons sugar
1 tablespoon fresh coriander, finely chopped

UTENSILS
A pressure cooker or deep pan with a lid

Method

1. Heat the oil and fry half the onions golden brown and almost crisp.

2. Add the rest of the onions with the curry leaves, chillies, ginger, and garlic. Fry for 5-6 minutes.

3. Add all the spices and salt and fry a few seconds more.

4. Add the mince and fry till its water evaporates and it gets lightly browned.

5. Add about a cup of hot water and the tomatoes. Close the cooker and allow it to reach maximum pressure. Reduce heat and keep on the fire about 10 minutes. Open the cooker, check that the mince is tenderised. Traditionally, this recipe has gravy, but you could decide whether you want it drier. (In case you are not pressure cooking, add more water and cook on a slow fire till done.)

6. Add the vinegar and sugar and adjust seasoning.

7. Serve garnished with the coriander.

Serves 6.

SINDHI KOFTE

Sindhi Meat Ball Curry.
Soft, melt-in-the-mouth koftas
simmered in a rich, curds curry.

INGREDIENTS

5 tablespoons cooking oil
3 cloves
A small stick of cinnamon
A bay leaf
3 large onions, ground
1½" piece of ginger, ground
5-6 cloves garlic, ground with the ginger
Green chillies to taste, chopped
2-3 teaspoons poppy seeds (optional), ground
3 tomatoes, pureed or blanched and chopped
¼ teaspoon turmeric powder
1 teaspoon coriander powder
Salt to taste
Black pepper to taste
1 cup milk
2 cups water
For the koftas
250 gms mince
3 tablespoons curds
A small piece of ginger, finely chopped or ground
Green chillies
Salt to taste
Fresh coriander, finely chopped

UTENSILS
A flat-bottomed pan with a lid

An electric grinder

Method
1. Heat the oil. Drop in the whole spices and bay leaf. Fry a minute.
2. Add the onions. Fry light brown.
3. Add the ginger and garlic. Fry golden brown.
4. Add the poppy seeds, if you're using it and the chillies. Fry a rich brown.
5. Add the tomatoes. Fry till the fat separates.
6. Add the spices—the turmeric, coriander, salt and pepper. Fry a few seconds.
7. Mix together the milk and water. Stirring continuously, off the fire, add it to the pan. Put the pan back on the fire and simmer till the gravy is thickened and reduced.
8. While the gravy is cooking you can make the *koftas*. Grind the mince with the curds and if you're grinding the ginger, the ginger.
9. Into the ground mixture, add the rest of the ingredients, mixing in well with the fin-   gertips.
10. Rub oil lightly on your palms. Take a little mixture, first press it together in one hand then shape into a ball about the size of a lemon. Use up all the mixture.

11. Gently slide the shaped *koftas* into the simmering gravy. Shut the pan tightly and cook on a slow fire. First, the meat will release its juices, then you will notice that the curry is drying up again. If needed, you might have to add a little water to help the *koftas* cook thoroughly. Also, shake the pan gently during the cooking process to ensure the *koftas* don't start sticking to the bottom. When the *koftas* are fully cooked, (which will take about half an hour) the fat will have separated and you should have a thick, clinging curry.

Serves 4.

SHIKAMPURI KABAB

Shikampuri Cutlets
A speciality that I associate with
sumptious Eid meals at a friend's house.

INGREDIENTS

500 gms mince, washed; ¼ cup Bengal gram;
10 cloves garlic; 4-5 green cardamoms,
pounded; 1 stick cinnamon; 3 cloves;
1 teaspoon black cumin; 2 tablespoons cooking
oil; ½ cup water; ½ cup almonds, blanched
and chopped; ½ cup fresh coconut, grated;
2 tablespoons lime juice; Chilli powder to taste
Salt to taste; ½ teaspoon turmeric powder;
2 eggs, lightly beaten; A few segments of orange
(when in season); Oil for frying

UTENSILS
A pressure cooker and a deep pan
An electric or manual grinder; Brown paper

Method

1. Into the pressure cooker, put the mince along with the next eight ingredients. Close the cooker and allow it to come to maximum pressure. Reduce heat and keep 10 minutes. Open the cooker—the mince should be cooked and completely dry. If it isn't, dry out any excess moisture.

2. Add the almonds and coconut. Fry till the moisture from the coconut also evaporates.

3. Cool the mixture and grind it in an electric or manual grinder to a fine paste.

4. Take it out of the grinder and add the lime juice, chilli powder, salt, turmeric and eggs. Mix together well.

5. Rub oil lightly on your palms. Divide the mixture into 8-10 portions. Shape each into a ball, then flatten gently. Poke a hole in the centre with your thumb. If oranges are in season, remove the threads, and the thin skin and use some of the orange pulp as filling. Reshape the *kabab* (If you are not using oranges, you can try chopped, hard-boiled eggs or mint and coriander, finely chopped). You can make the *kababs* circular or tear-drop shaped.

6. When you're ready to eat, heat the oil. Since you have to deep fry, you will need at least half a panful. Bring the oil to smoking point, then reduce heat and wait 5 minutes. Drop the *kababs* in in batches and fry till they're a even golden brown on all sides. Drain on brown paper before serving.

Makes 8-10 largeish ones.

Note: You can make smaller kababs if you prefer.

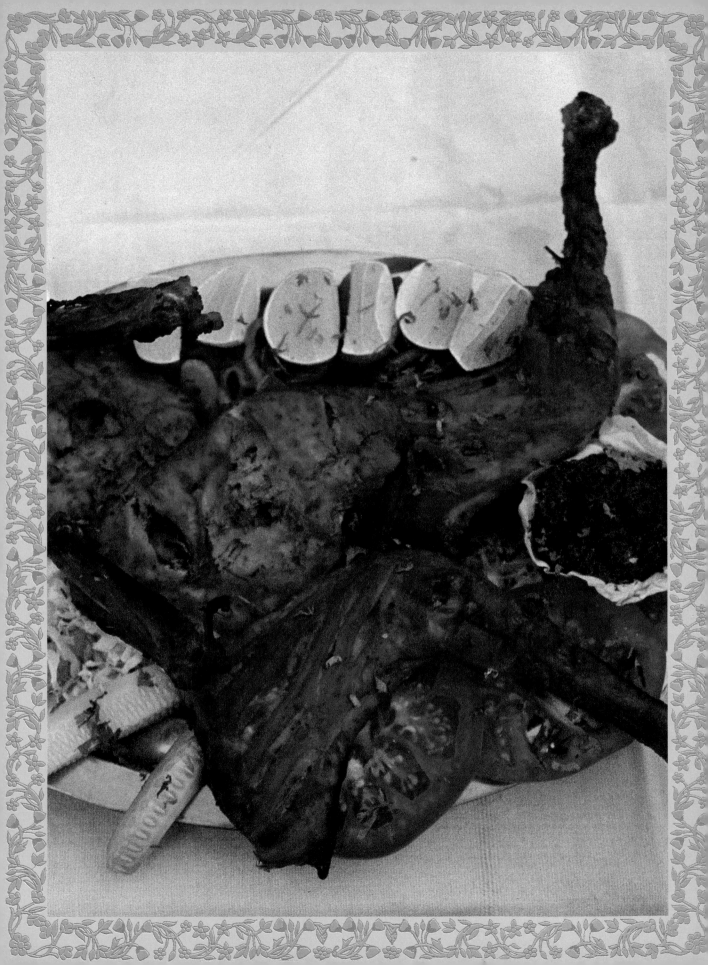

NIMBUWALI MURGHI

Chicken Flavoured with Lemon.
The lemon flavouring is only part of the
story. This absolutely mouth-watering
chicken is marinated and cooked in curds,
then fried to a tender crispness.

INGREDIENTS

1 chicken, weighing about 900 gms, cleaned
and jointed
$^3/_4$ cups slightly sour curds
2 small onions, ground
1 whole pod garlic, ground
$1^1/_2$" piece of ginger, ground
2 teaspoons coriander powder
Red chilli powder to taste
Salt to taste
2 onions
Vinegar
$^1/_2$ teaspoon sugar
$^1/_2$ teaspoon salt
1 cup cooking oil
Juice of $1^1/_2$ limes
$1^1/_2$ tablespoons fresh coriander leaves, finely
chopped

UTENSILS

A heavy-bottomed pan
Another, preferably flat-bottomed skillet to fry
in and Brown paper

Method

1. Pierce each piece of chicken well with
a fork.

2. Mix together the next seven ingredients.
This is the marinade. Rub it well into each
piece of chicken, pour any excess over and leave
to marinate at least 8 hours or, if
possible, overnight.

3. Separately, slice 2 onions in thin rings and soak
in enough vinegar to just cover them. Mix in the
salt and sugar. Keep aside. They will turn a
delicate pink.

4. Put the chicken along with the marinade into
a pan, cover and cook on a slow fire till the
chicken has cooked through and the liquids
have all dried up. You might need to uncover the
pan and boil rapidly to achieve this, in the last
ten minutes.

5. Heat the oil in the skillet. Fry the pieces of
chicken in batches till lightly browned all over.
Drain on the brown paper.

6. Put the pieces on a serving plate and pour a
little lime juice over each.

7. Serve garnished with the onion rings and
fresh coriander.

Serves 4.

MURGH MAKHANI

Butter Chicken.
A relatively simple recipe for
this popular speciality.

INGREDIENTS

1 medium chicken, weighing about 900 gms,
washed and jointed
FOR THE MARINADE
4 tablespoons slightly sour curds, lightly beaten;
Juice of 1 small lime; 2 teaspoons ground garlic;
2 teaspoons grated or ground ginger;
Red chilli powder to taste; 1 teaspoon coriander
powder; Salt to taste; 4 tablespoons oil
FOR THE SAUCE
500 gms tomatoes, chopped; 2 tablespoons fresh
chopped coriander; 1" piece of ginger, peeled and
chopped; Green chillies to taste; A pinch of
turmeric; 1 tablespoon tomato sauce (optional); 1
teaspoon sugar; A generous dash of black
pepper;³/₄ cup cream or top-of-the-milk; ¹/₂ teaspoon
garam masala; ¹/₂ teaspoon cumin powder

UTENSILS
A heavy-bottomed pan to cook the chicken
Another pan to cook the sauce

Method

1. Mix together the curds, lime juice, garlic,
ginger, chilli, coriander and salt. This is the
marinade. Make gashes or prick holes all over
the pieces of chicken and rub in the curd

mixture well. It is best to do this with your
fingers. Keep aside for as many hours as you can
or overnight if possible.

2. Heat the oil in the pan. Put in the chicken,
cover the pan and let it cook till it is fully
tenderised. The liquids should all evaporate and
the chicken should get lightly fried in the oil
remaining in the pan.

3. While the chicken is cooking, you can make
the sauce. Puree together all the ingredients for
the sauce except the last three.

4. Lightly beat half the cream and stir it into the
pureed mixture. Set it on a slow fire. Cook till
the fat separates.

5. Slip the pieces of chicken into the simmering
sauce and let them heat through thoroughly.

6. Just before you're ready to serve, gently stir in
the rest of the cream and sprinkle over the
cumin and *garam masala*.

Serves 4.

Note: If you prefer, you may cook the chicken
in an oven. Preheat it to 150°C/300°F. Put the
chicken in an oven-proof dish with a lid (or
covered with foil) and cook till done. Remove
the lid or foil in the last 10 minutes.

DHANSAK

Chicken with Pulses and Vegetables.
The famous Parsi speciality, that,
apart from being an ingenious blend
of flavours, is very wholesome too.

INGREDIENTS

1 chicken weighing about 900 gms
3 tablespoons each Split Red Gram, Whole
Green Gram and Lentils, picked and washed
1 small long brinjal, chopped; A handful fresh
fenugreek leaves, washed and chopped
100 grams each red and white pumpkin,
chopped; 2 potatoes, peeled and diced;
2 onions, chopped; Salt to taste; $^1/_2$ teaspoon
turmeric powder
4-5 tablespoons cooking oil; 2-3 spring onions
(include some greens) or 1 large onion, chopped
fine; $^1/_2$ teaspoon whole fenugreek seeds
1 teaspoon cumin; 2 teaspoons coriander
powder; $1^1/_2$" piece of ginger, ground wit
5-6 cloves garlic, ground; 1 tablespoon dhansak
powder;
Lime-sized ball of tamarind, soaked in $1^1/_2$ cups
water
2 teaspoons jaggery, soaked along with the
tamarind

UTENSILS

A heavy-bottomed pan with a lid
A bowl to soak the tamarind
An electric or manual blender
An extra pan to make the tempering

Method

1. Put the chicken, pulses, vegetables, turmeric and salt into the pan. Add enough water
to just cover all the ingredients, then cover th pan and cook on a slow fire till all the ingredients are tenderised. This should take 30-45 minutes depending on the quality of the chicken.

2. Take off the fire and from the pan, remove all the pieces of chicken. Keep aside for the moment.

3. Puree the rest of the ingredients, then pour back over the chicken.

4. Heat the oil in the second pan. Add the onions. Fry golden brown. Remove half of them and reserve for the garnish. To the ones remaining in the pan, add all the seeds, coriander, ginger, garlic and the *dhansak* powder. Fry, stirring almost continuously.

5. Pour this tempering over the chicken and blend well. Allow the whole mixture to come to a boil.

6. Meanwhile, extract the pulp from the soaked tamarind, discard the seeds and add this liquid to the simmering chicken. Simmer 10 minutes.

7. Serve garnished with the reserved onions.
Serves 6-8.

MURGHI VINDALOO

Chicken Goan Style.
The hot, sweet and sour taste of Goa. This recipe
uses a medium-hot Vindaloo powder. If you
prefer a milder version, tone down the chillies.
Also, avoid the green chillies, but don't ask Goans
for their comments!

INGREDIENTS

1 tablespoon Vindaloo *powder (see Glossary)*
1½" *piece of ginger, ground*
7-8 cloves garlic, ground
1 chicken, weighing about 900 gms, washed
and jointed
6 tablespoons mustard oil
2 bay leaves
5 green cardamoms, pounded
2 large onions, sliced finely
Salt to taste
Green chillies to taste, chopped or sliced
Water
1 tablespoon tamarind, soaked in about ½ cup
water
1-2 teaspoons vinegar
1-2 teaspoons sugar

UTENSILS

A heavy-bottomed pan with a lid
A small bowl to soak the tamarind
A bowl or plate to marinate the chicken

Method

1. Mix together the *Vindaloo* powder, ginger and garlic. This is the marinade.
2. Prick the chicken all over with a fork. Rub the marinade all over, rubbing in well with the fingers. Keep aside for at least half an hour and longer if possible.
3. Heat the oil. Drop the bay leaves into it.
4. After a few seconds, add the cardamoms. Let them fry for another few seconds.
5. Add the onions. Fry light brown.
6. Add the chicken. Fry along with the marinade till lightly browned all over.
7. Add salt, chillies and water. About 2 cups should be sufficient. Stir, cover the pan and cook on a slow fire till the chicken is tenderised and the curry reduced. This should take 30-45 minutes, depending on the quality of the chicken.
8. Push the pulp of the tamarind through a strainer. Discard the seeds and add the pulp to the chicken in the pan. Simmer 5 minutes.
9. Add the vinegar and sugar. Check the seasoning, particularly the blend of sour and sweet and add sugar or vinegar as needed.

Serves 4.

Note: This recipe can also be used to cook any meat or even more typical of Goan cooking, pork.

HARE MASALE KI MURGHI

Chicken in a Green Sauce.
This unusual chicken incorporates 4
green flavours. It's a winning
combination all right, especially if all
the leaves are fresh.

INGREDIENTS

5 tablespoons cooking oil
1 whole red chilli
2 black cardamoms, pounded
A small stick of cinnamon
1 bay leaf
2 onions, ground
1 teaspoon ground ginger
1 teaspoon ground garlic
Green chillies to taste, chopped
3 tablespoons spinach, washed and ground
3 tablespoons fenugreek leaves, washed and
ground
3 tablespoons dill, washed and ground
4 tablespoons coriander leaves. washed and
ground
1 medium chicken, weighing about 900 gms
jointed and washed
Salt to taste
3-4 tablespoons cream, lightly beaten
A dash of sugar

UTENSILS
A deep pan with a lid

Method

1. Heat the oil. Drop in the chilli. Discard it
when it darkens completely.
2. Put into the hot oil the cardamoms, cinnamon,
and bay leaf. Fry a few seconds.
3. Add the onions. Fry light brown.
4. Add the ginger and garlic. Fry golden brown,
adding a few teaspoons of water during the
process, if required.
5. Add all the greens and chillies. Fry 5 minutes.
6. Add the chicken and salt. Cover and cook till
the chicken is tenderised. If there are any excess
liquids, boil them away.
7. Just before serving, heat the chicken through
and gently stir in the cream and sugar. Serve
immediately.

Serves 4.

MURGH MALAI KABAB

Creamy Bonless Chicken.
These juicy bits of chicken are as melt-in-the
mouth as kababs *can possibly be. This is the way*
they are made in the Bukhara at Delhi,
acknowledged as one of the finest restaurants for
Tandoori food.

INGREDIENTS

12 breasts of chicken, dressed
$^1/_2$ teaspoon ground ginger
6 teaspoons ground garlic
1 teaspoon white pepper powder
Salt to taste
THE MARINADE
1 egg, lightly beaten
$^1/_2$ cup grated cheese, preferably Cheddar
8 green chillies, deseeded and finely chopped
2-3 tablespoons fresh coriander, finely chopped
2/3 cup cream, lightly beaten
$^1/_2$ teaspoon nutmeg powder
$^1/_2$ teaspoon mace powder
3 tablespoons cornflour
Butter for basting

UTENSILS
A bowl to marinate the chicken
Skewers
An oven tray

Method
1. Debone the chicken and cut each breast into two pieces.

2. Mix together the ginger, garlic, pepper and salt, and rub into the chicken. Keep aside for 15 minutes.

3. Whisk together all the ingredients for the marinade. Rub all over the chicken and keep aside for at least 3 hours. If the temperatures are very high, it is a good idea to keep it in the refrigerator.

4. Just before you're ready to cook, preheat the oven to 140°C (275°F)

5. Skewer the pieces of chicken an inch apart. Put into the oven. Keep a tray underneath to collect the drippings. It is less messy if you line the tray with aluminium foil. Keep in the oven for 6 minutes, then remove and balance the skewers horizontally, each end on an upturned glass or bowl. Keep a tray below it to allow the excess moisture to drip off into it, baste with a little butter and put back into the oven for another 3 minutes or till done.

Makes 24 kababs.

TANDOORI POMFRET

Baked Pomfret,
Another Bukhara speciality and just as
mouth-watering as the last recipe.

INGREDIENTS
4 pomfrets, each weighing about 450 gms

THE MARINADE
¹/₄ cup curds
2 egg yolks
3 tablespoons cream, lightly beaten
3¹/₂ teaspoons ground ginger
3¹/₂ teaspoons ground garlic
4 teaspoons thymol seeds (ajwain)
2 tablespoons gramflour
¹/₂ teaspoon white pepper
Salt to taste
2 teaspoons chilli powder
2 tablespoons lemon juice
1 teaspoon turmeric powder
Butter for basting

UTENSILS
A plate to marinate the fish
Skewers
An oven tray to collect the drippings
A muslin cloth or strainer

Method
1. Clean and wash the fish and make 3 deep incisions across each side.
2. Hang the curds in a muslin cloth or put into a strainer for about 15 minutes to drain the whey. Mix in the rest of the ingredients for the marinade.
3. Rub the fish all over with the marinade and keep aside for at least 3 hours. If you are doing this in very hot weather, keep the fish in the refrigerator.
4. When you're ready to cook, pre-heat the oven to 180°C (350°F).
5. Skewer the fish. On a normal-sized skewer, you should be able to comfortably fit one fish. The skewer passes through the centre of the fish, from mouth to tail. If you have a rotating grill you should be able to cook all the fish simultaneously.
6. Put into the oven. Put the tray, preferably lined with aluminium foil, underneath.
7. Keep in the oven 12 minutes, then remove from the oven and balance the skewers horizontally, each of the two edges on a bowl or upturned glass to allow the excess fat to drip away. Keep a tray underneath to catch the dripping. Baste with the butter and put back into the oven for 3 minutes or till done.

Makes 4 large servings.

RAI MACHCHI

Mustard Fish.
A sharp and delicious Bengali blend
of flavours. If you enjoy the taste of
mustard, you will love this.

INGREDIENTS

500 gms fresh hilsa, tangra, pabda, *herring or*
rohu, *cleaned and washed*
2-3 tablespoons sharp mustard powder
2 glasses water
$^1/_2$ teaspoon turmeric powder
Salt to taste
4 tablespoons mustard oil
1 teaspoon onion seeds
3 onions, finely chopped
3-4 green chillies, chopped
2 teaspoons mustard oil

UTENSILS
Any heavy-bottomed pan with a lid

Method

1. Dissolve the mustard powder in the water and
add to it the turmeric and salt. Keep aside for at
least half an hour to allow the flavour to mature.

2. Meanwhile, heat the oil to smoking point, then
reduce heat and wait 5 minutes. Drop in the
onion seeds. Stir.

3. After a few seconds, add the onions. Fry
golden brown.

4. Pour in the mustard water and bring to boil.

5. Gently slip in the fish, cover and cook
5-7 minutes.

6. Check that the fish is cooked, then add the
chillies, cover the pan again and keep on the fire
another 2 minutes.

7. Before the fire is turned off, stir in the
fresh oil.

Serves 4.

Note: You can use any fleshy fish for this
recipe.

134

METHI
MACHCHI

Fenugreek Fish.
A superb, Sindhi blend of
flavours—fish smothered in a
green, fenugreek curry.

INGREDIENTS

Pomfret, or any other fish, weighing about 500
gms, well-washed and cut in pieces
5 tablespoons cooking oil
1 teaspoon cumin seeds
2 medium onions, ground
³/₄ cup chopped, fresh or 4-5 teaspoons dried
fenugreek leaves
Green chillies to taste
A small bunch of fresh coriander leaves
4-5 cloves garlic
1" piece of ginger
¹/₂ teaspoon turmeric powder
1 teaspoon coriander powder
1 teaspoon sugar
2-3 tomatoes, pureed
Salt to taste

UTENSILS
A pan with a lid
A griddle

Method

1. Heat the oil and lightly fry the fish. Remove and keep aside.
2. In the same oil (add a little more if needed), add the cumin seeds. Don't allow them to get too dark.
3. Add the onions and fry golden brown.
4. Grind together the fenugreek, chillies, coriander, garlic and ginger and add with the rest of the ingredients. Cook a few minutes.
5. Add the fish, stir well, cover and cook 5 minutes, then put the griddle underneath and continue cooking till tender—about 7-10 minutes. By this time, the curry should have thickened and be clinging to the fish. During the cooking process, you may need to add a little water (¹/₂-1 cup) so check before you put the griddle underneath.

Serves 4.

DAHI
MACHCHI

Fish Cooked in Curds.
Mustard oil and curds bring to this
recipe authentic Bengali flavours and
finesse. This is best eaten with plain,
boiled rice.

INGREDIENTS

500 gms hilsa, bekti *or any fleshy fish, cleaned*
and cut in pieces
$^1/_2$ teaspoon turmeric powder
$^1/_2$ teaspoon salt
$^1/_2$ cup mustard oil
2 bay leaves
Green chillies to taste, sliced lengthwise
2 onions, ground
1" piece of ginger, ground
$^1/_2$ cup curds, lightly beaten
$^1/_2$-1 teaspoon sugar
$^1/_2$ cup water
1 teaspoon ghee *or melted butter*
$^1/_2$ teaspoon garam masala

UTENSILS
A heavy bottomed pan with a lid

Method

1. Mix together the salt and turmeric and rub all
over the fish pieces. Keep aside for half an hour.

2. Heat the oil to smoking point, then reduce
heat and wait 5 minutes. Slip the pieces of fish
into the oil and fry till golden brown. Remove
and keep aside.

3. In the same oil (remove the excess,
leaving only 4-5 tablespoons in the pan),
add the bay leaves and green chillies. Fry a
few seconds.

4. Add the onion and fry light brown.

5. Add the ginger and stirring continuously, fry
till golden brown.

6. Add the curds and sugar and mix well.

7. Add the fish pieces and coat each well with
the mixture in the pan. Check salt, adding more
if needed.

8. Add $^1/_2$ cup water. Blend in well, then cover the
pan and simmer fish gently over low heat till
fully cooked.

9. Before serving, stir in the *ghee* or butter and
sprinkle over the *garam masala*.

Serves 4.

PRAWN
BALCHAO

Prawns Goan style.
An authentic recipe for this piquant
preparation from Goa. Though
traditionally fiery, I have left it to you to
decide how hot you want to make it.

INGREDIENTS

2 teaspoons cumin powder

2 teaspoons mustard seeds

1½ teaspoons pepper, freshly ground

Red chilli powder to taste

1 teaspoon turmeric powder

Salt to taste

500 gms prawns, deveined and washed

½ cup cooking oil

4 large onions, finely chopped

15 cloves garlic, finely chopped

2" piece of ginger, finely chopped

15 curry leaves, washed and torn up

Vinegar to taste

UTENSILS

A largeish heavy-bottomed pan with a lid.

Method

1. Grind the cumin and mustard with a little vinegar.
2. Mix with pepper, chilli, turmeric and salt and sprinkle and rub into the prawns. Keep aside.

3. Meanwhile, heat the oil. Bring it to smoking point, then reduce heat and wait 5 minutes.
4. Drop in the chopped onions. Fry till lightly browned.
5. Add the garlic and stirring frequently, fry till the fat just starts to separate.
6. Add the prawns, ginger and curry leaves. Cover and cook till the prawns are done and the fat is separating.
7. Add the vinegar—how much you need depends on how sour you want it. Check seasoning too and add more salt if needed. Continue cooking till the fat has all floated to the top.

Note: How many this recipe serves depends on how fiery you make it and whether you eat it as a sort of pickle or otherwise as an accompaniment to a meal. In the latter case, I would remove most of the excess oil. You can expect it to serve 4-6 people. You may also cook any other fish this way.

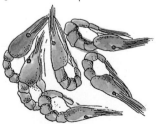

137

COOLING CURDS
REFRESHING RELISHES

CURDS
&
RELISHES

This penultimate section brings to you recipes for those extra touches that go towards making your meal complete. There are curds (yogurt) to start with, that not only make a wholesome suppliment to any menu but are also a cooling counterpoint to spicy, rich curries. Teamed with *pullaos*—rice cooked with meat or vegetables—they make a satisfying, complete meal. *Raitas,* curds which have been tempered or to which vegetables and spices have been added, make an even more interesting addition. There are some tempting ones here—a mint-flavoured one to which you can add potatoes, a pale green, pleasant combination of cucumber with curds, a more perky variation tempered with mustard seeds and an unusual recipe which I got during a visit to the Kumaon hills. This one also uses mustard seeds, though not fried as in the last recipe, but ground to impart a sharp, piquant twist to the normally mild-mannered curds. The section wouldn't be complete without the very special Fritters in Curds *(Dahi-Pakoris).* I must admit these take a few trials to master. I made them a number of times before I perfected them and managed to make them as melt-in-the mouth as I thought they should be. I have tried to make the recipe as precise as possible so that you can be successful the first time round.

Apart from all these variations, you can serve curds plain of course though in that case, take extra care to ensure they are well set. This means they should be neither too sour, nor too watery and tasteless. The temperature of the milk you use, and the amount of starter (day-old curds) you add depends on the weather. In summer you need to just barely warm the milk and add less than a teaspoonful of the starter for a bowlful that contains about 2 cups milk. The best way to do it is to mix the curds with a little whey to a smooth paste so you can stir it evenly into the milk. Cover the bowl and leave in a dry place to set, for at least 5 hours. Of course, in the hot weather, you can set curds in 3 hours too by heating the milk more, and by adding a little more starter but I personally feel it's not as flavourful as the one which is allowed to sit for a longer time. In winter, you have a different problem on hand. The curds will not set unless they're pampered and kept warm. The milk must be hotter to start with, the quantity of starter used must be doubled, and the curds must be left to set in a warm, draught-free corner, preferably in a cupboard, covered with a warm cloth. A tea cosy or a woollen cap is most convenient. Even then you can expect that the curds will take longer to set. Once it's done however, it's important to refrigerate it otherwise the curds will start exuding water and become too sour.

You might like to add a teaspoon or so of sugar to the warmed milk before setting the curds, if you prefer them slightly sweetened.

Apart from curds, in this section you have recipes for some quick chutneys. Refreshing mint, sweet and sour tamarind, chewy coconut are sure to enliven and add interest to any menu, as will the lemony ginger relish, which is so easy to make and get addicted to.

DAHI
RAI
WALA

Curds Tempered with Mustard Seeds.
A delicious study in contrasts—cool
curds with a spicy tempering.

INGREDIENTS
4 cups curds, lightly beaten
Salt and pepper to taste
Green chillies to taste, deseeded and chopped
1 tablespoon cooking oil
1 teaspoon mustard seeds
A few curry leaves
1 tomato, finely chopped

UTENSILS
A bowl for the curds
A small pan to make the tempering

Method
1. Into the curds, add the salt and pepper.

2. Fold in the green chillies.
3. Heat the oil. Drop in the mustard seeds. Let them splutter.
4. Add the tomato and torn-up curry leaves. Fry, stirring almost continuously, till the fat separates.
5. Pour over the curds, stir in gently and refrigerate till needed.

Serves 4-5.

Note: You can add boiled and cubed potatoes to this too, to make the dish more substantial. For 4 persons, in that case, 2 ½ cup curds and 3 potatoes should be sufficient.

ALU RAITA

Minted Curds with Potatoes.
A pleasantly cool
counterpoint to any meal.
The fresh flavour of mint is
most refreshing.

INGREDIENTS

3 medium potatoes, boiled

2 ½ cups curds, lightly beaten

1 ½ tablespoons fresh coriander, chopped

1 ½ tablespoon fresh mint, chopped

1 clove garlic (optional)

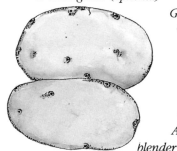

Green chillies to taste, deseeded and chopped

Salt to taste

Sugar to taste

UTENSILS

An electric or manual blender

A bowl to whisk the curds

Method

1. Cool the potatoes completely, preferably for a few hours after boiling, then peel and cube them. Drop into the curds.

2. Grind the coriander, mint and garlic, if you are using it.

3. Mix the ground paste, chillies, the sugar and salt into the curds. Check the seasoning, and refrigerate till needed.

Serves 4.

Note: You need not use potatoes. Even the minted curds by themselves taste delicious, though of course, you will need an additional cup of curds to serve four.

PAHADI RAITA

Mustard Flavoured Curds.
A piquant, lemon coloured
preparation. Apart from
serving it at a meal, you
could use it as a dip too.

INGREDIENTS
4 cups curds, lightly beaten
2 teaspoons mustard seeds, ground
Salt to taste
Green chillies to taste, chopped finely
A touch of sugar (optional)

UTENSILS
A grinder
A bowl

Method
1. Mix all the ingredients into the curds. Don't add all the mustard all at once. Add half of it and then taste to see exactly how much you want to add. Remember too that the flavour will accentuate with keeping. Ideally, you should do the mixing and refrigerate the mixture at least 3-4 hours before serving. A little extra mustard can always be added at the last minute too.

Serves 4-5.

Note: Cucumber can be added to this raita too. The proportions would be the same as for the Curds with Cucumber.

KHEERE KA RAITA

*Curds with Cucumber.
Well-chilled and seasoned,
there's nothing to beat this
cooling combination on a
hot summers day.*

INGREDIENTS
3 cups curds, lightly beaten
Salt to taste
Sugar to taste
1 cup cucumber, chopped very fine or grated
Green chillies to taste, chopped fine
2 teaspoons fresh soya, finely chopped

(if in season);

1-1¼ teaspoons cumin powder

UTENSILS
A colander to drain the cucumber
A bowl to whisk the curds

Method
1. Season the curds with the salt and sugar.

2. Sprinkle salt over the cucumber and leave
to drain in the colander. Keep aside for
at least 15 minutes then gently squeeze and fold
into the curds.
3. Stir in the soya and chillies. Refrigerate till
needed.
4. Sprinkle over cumin powder before serving.

Serves 4.

*Note: If you are not averse to the taste of fresh
ginger, it makes for a wonderful addition to
this raita. Cube a few teaspoons minutely and
add it.*

MOOLI
KA
RAITA

*Curds with Radish.
The radish loses its
pungency as it mingles with
the curds in a most
harmonious combination.
It is best made when the
radish is really fresh.*

INGREDIENTS

3 cups curds, lightly beaten
Salt to taste
Red chilli powder to taste
Black pepper to taste
Sugar to taste
1 cup radish, peeled and grated
1 teaspoon cumin powder

UTENSILS

A colander to drain the radish
A bowl to whisk the curds

Method

1. Into the curds, mix in and adjust the seasonings.
2. Sprinkle a little salt over the radish and leave to drain in a colander for at least 15-20 minutes. Squeeze gently between the palms, to remove all excess moisture before adding to the curds.
3. Garnish with the cumin and refrigerate till needed.

Serves 4.

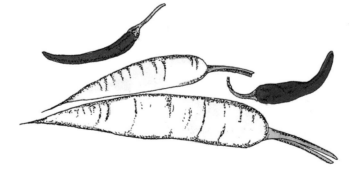

BOONDIWALI DAHI

Curds with Gramflour Drops.
In this unique combination, gramflour is made into a
thickish batter and pressed through a slotted spoon or
special gadget so that it falls into hot oil in the shape of
tiny drops. These are fried, drained and then added to
seasoned curds. It makes a wholesome addition to any
menu. If you don't want to make them at home, you can
buy the boondis *at any good grocery or sweetmeat store.*

INGREDIENTS
3 cups curds, lightly beaten
3 tablespoons boondis
Hot water

Salt and red chilli powder to taste
1 teaspoon cumin powder
Fresh coriander, finely
chopped

UTENSILS
A small bowl to soak the
boondis
A bowl to whisk the curds

Method
1. Soak the *boondis* in the water in the bowl. If
they are not salted, you can add some salt to the
water. They will puff up slightly. Leave them in
water for about 15 minutes then squeeze them
gently between your palms and drop them into
the curds.
2. Add the rest of the ingredients.
3. Refrigerate till needed.
4. Stir well before serving.

Serves 4.

DAHI PAKORI

Fritters in Curds.
The most elaborate of the curds-based
preparations, this takes some effort to
practice but truly, it is well worth the effort.
Soft, melt-in-the-mouth fritters will never fail
to win you compliments.

INGREDIENTS

1 cup White Gram picked, washed and soaked
overnight
A pinch of baking soda
2-3 cups oil
2 cups hot water
1 teaspoon salt
4 cups curds, lightly beaten
Salt, sugar and red chilli powder to taste
1½ -2 teaspoons cumin powder
Green chillies, sliced

UTENSILS

A bowl to beat the batter; An electric or manual
grinder; An electric beater; A deep pan to fry
the fritters; A bowl to whisk the curds; Brown
paper; A small bowl for the water

Method

1. Grind the gram, in an electric or manual
grinder, with a few tablespoons water. It should
become a smooth paste.
2. Remove from the grinder and with a metal
spoon, or electric beater beat till the batter
becomes very light. At this stage add the baking
soda. If the batter is too thick add just a little

water to make the task easier. Keep a small
bowl filled with water near by. The batter is
done when a spoonful dropped into the water
floats. Keep aside for another few hours if you
have the time.
3. Heat the oil to smoking point, then reduce
heat and wait 5 minutes. Drop spoonfuls of the
batter into the oil, in batches, frying to an even
golden brown. Test the first batch to see if it's
getting done correctly—the fritters should get
brown and get cooked thoroughly. Drain them
on brown paper.
4. When all the fritters are done, drop them into
the water to which the salt has been added.
Keep each batch in it for about five minutes then
take out, squeeze gently between the palms and
lay in a flat serving dish.
5. Season the curds. Pour a little more than half
over the fritters and refrigerate.
6. Just before you're ready to eat, pour the
remaining curds over and garnish with a sprinkle
of cumin powder, some sliced green chillies, and
lashings of Tamarind Chutney
(see recipe ahead).
Serves 6-8 (makes about 20-24 large lemon
sized fritters).

NARIYAL KI CHUTNEY

Coconut Chutney.
A soothing, almost chewy chutney that
is best served at room temperature.

INGREDIENTS

¹/₂ coconut
2 tablespoons cooking oil
1 slightly heaped tablespoon Bengal Gram
Green chillies to taste, chopped
1" piece of ginger, peeled and chopped
5 tablespoons fresh coriander, chopped
Juice of 2 limes
Salt to taste
1 teaspoon mustard seeds.

UTENSILS

An electric or manual grinder
A coconut grater

Method

1. Carefully break the coconut. Be careful not to let the water get wasted. Keep it aside. Grate the pulp from the coconut. The task is made easier if you have a coconut scraper. This is a ball shaped gadget, with a number of serrated edges (made to fit inside a half coconut) which fit on a rod to a stand. The stand sticks onto your counter top as you rotate the handle and the pulp is grated out quite easily.

2. Heat the oil in a small pan. Drop the gram into it and fry till light brown. Don't overfry, or your chutney will be bitter. Drain the gram and keep the oil aside for the moment.

3. Into the grinder, put the grated coconut, gram and the rest of the ingredients except the mustard seeds. Put in as much of the coconut water as you think you need to help you liquidise it easily and get a paste of the consistency you want. You would do well to keep it a little thinner than the final consistency you like since it tends to absorb moisture as it sits. Adjust seasoning and pour the chutney out into a bowl.

4. Of the reserved oil, keep just a tablespoon in the pan. Heat it. Drop in the mustard seeds. As soon as they stop spluttering, pour them over the chutney and mix in well.

5. Refrigerate till a little while before you intend to serve it.

Makes 1 cup.

PUDINE KI CHUTNEY

Mint Chutney.
It goes with snacks; it goes with
all kinds of menus; it is a
refreshing dip or sandwich
spread. You would do well to
make a cupful whenever you can

INGREDIENTS
1 ¹/₂ cups packed fresh mint, chopped
1 ¹/₂ cups packed fresh coriander, chopped
Green chillies to taste, chopped
Juice of 1-1 ¹/₂ limes
1 teaspoon sugar or to taste
Salt to taste
1 clove garlic
A small piece of ginger, peeled and chopped
(optional)

UTENSILS
An electric or manual grinder

Method
1. Put all the ingredients into the grinder. Put as little water as possible. Grind to a smooth paste. Taste and adjust seasoning. Chill till required.

Makes about 1 cup.

Note: When green mangoes are in season, add 1 small one to the ingredients. You can cut down on the lemon juice. You can also try adding roasted and ground pomegranate seeds which other than imparting sourness, also add a delightful texture to the chutney.

152

AMBAL

*Mango Chutney.
A thin, liquidy, sweet-sour
chutney from Bengal. Well
chilled, it is most welcome on a
hot day, particularly when rice
and pulses are on the menu.*

INGREDIENTS
*4 medium-sized green mangoes, washed and
skinned
4 teaspoons mustard oil
2 whole red chillies, broken and deseeded
1 teaspoon mustard seeds
4 dessertspoons sugar
Salt to taste
4 cups water
Vinegar (optional)*

UTENSILS
A heavy-bottomed pan

Method
1. Cut the mangoes into thin strips. Discard the seeds.
2. Heat the oil and drop in the red chillies.
3. After a few seconds, add the mustard seeds. As soon as they stop spluttering, add the mango. Fry lightly for about five minutes.
4. Add the sugar and salt and continue cooking and stirring till the sugar turns brownish.
5. Add the water and bring to boil. Check the taste after a few minutes. Add sugar or a little vinegar, if you feel the chutney is not sour enough. Reduce heat and simmer 10 minutes before taking off the fire.
6. Chill well before serving.

Makes about 5 cups.

IMLI KI CHUTNEY

Tamarind Chutney.
A dark brown, sweet-sour chutney that
adds zest to fritters and chaat *and*
provides the perfect finishing touch to
fritters in curds

INGREDIENTS

60 grams deseeded tamarind
90 grams jaggery
1¼ cups water
1 small onion, finely chopped
Green chillies to taste, finely chopped
1 tablespoon fresh coriander, finely chopped
1-1½ teaspoons ginger, finely chopped or
shredded
1 small tomato, finely chopped
Salt to taste
¼ teaspoon cumin powder (optional)

UTENSILS
2 bowls
Strainer

Method
1. Soak the tamarind and jaggery in the water.
Keep till the tamarind gets pulpy and the
jaggery gets dissolved. Push the jaggery and
pulp through a strainer. It will now be of a
slightly thinner consistency than what you
eventually want.
2. Put it on the fire. Cook and stir till it becomes
like a thick custard. This will take about 10
minutes.
3. Take off the fire, and add the rest of the
ingredients.
4. Refrigerate till needed.

Makes 1 cup.

Note: For a variation, add to the tamarind
mixture, while it is on the fire, black pepper to
taste, ½ teaspoon dried ginger powder, ½
teaspoon ground cumin, black salt to taste and
1 tablespoon raisins. Check seasonings and
remove from fire. Omit all other ingredients
mentioned above.

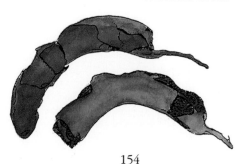

ADRAK NIMBU MEIN

Ginger Slices in Lemon.
These crunchy, lemony, ginger slices are not
only a piquant accompaniment to a meal,
they are a good digestive too. Eat them as
often as you can.

INGREDIENTS
A large piece (about 100 grams) of ginger
Juice of 4-5 lemons

UTENSILS
A small bowl
A glass jar

Method
1. Peel the ginger and slice into thin sticks. The best way to do this is to cut it first in thinnish slices, then cut the slices further into strips. Put into the glass jar.
2. Pour the juice over the lemon slices. Push the slices down so that most of them are covered by the juice. Keep the jar aside. The relish is ready to eat when the ginger slices turn pinkish. This relish is best eaten soon after it is ready—it will not keep for more than a week. Even for that period it is best kept in the refrigerator.

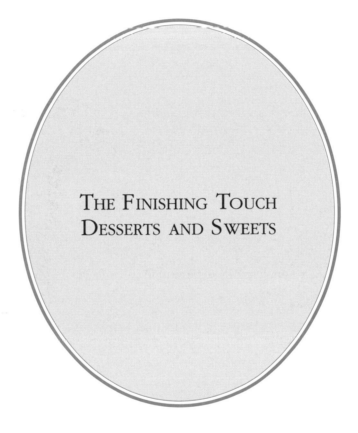

THE FINISHING TOUCH
DESSERTS AND SWEETS

DESSERTS & SWEETS

Indian desserts are traditionally rich and heavy on sugar. Perhaps this has something to do with their being associated with festive occasions, when serving something sweet is *de riguer*, the appropriate and auspicious thing to do.

Most festivals are times to exchange boxes of sweetmeats and perhaps the time you wait longest in a queue to buy them is when *Diwali* comes around. *Pongal*, the harvest festival in Tamil Nadu, would be unthinkable without *kheer*, a sweet in which rice is simmered in milk to a thick creamy, consistency and served garnished with nuts. Similarly, during the Ganapati festival, celebrated in Maharashtra, *laddoos*, ball-shaped sweets, usually made of *dal* are savoured and if you go to greet Muslim friends on *Eid-ul-Fitr*, fast before you do because you're in for a marathon session of tasting rich vermicelli sweets of many kinds. Semolina, *sooji*, comes into its own on *Nauroz*, the Parsi New Year's Day, and as far as Bengali sweets are concerned, they are indeed in a class apart, and popular all over the country. It is not only festivals, in fact, that call for sweets. Any happy occasion—the birth of a baby, a marriage announcement, news of a successful graduation, a promotion, and it is time to *muh meetha karo*, literally translated as sweeten the mouth.

Many Indian sweets, as you will notice from this section too, are milk based. The secret of rich, creamy *Kheer*, *Phirni* or for that matter, *Rabri*, is the temperature at which the milk simmers, and gets reduced or thickened. It must be done at low heat, with constant stirring to get perfect results. In themselves there is nothing complicated about the recipes but don't expect to hurry through them either. *Gajrela*, for example, the delectable combination of carrots and milk needs no particular expertise to make but it does require time. *Rasgullas* are another matter. To make really spongy, melt-in-the mouth ones needs some practice. The milk must be curdled correctly, the green whey completely separating from the cheese, which must then be kneaded or otherwise processed to an absolutely smooth paste and you have the basic ingredients for professional *Rasgullas*. I guess I could say exactly the same thing for *Sandesh*.

At the end of the section, I have included some fudge-like preparations—one flavoured with cashewnuts and another made with gramflour. You could try serving them for a change, after dinner or even tea. I didn't mention earlier that apart from festivals, and other happy occasions, sweets are very comfortable at the evening tea-table too!

Having said all that about the Indian sweet tooth, I must admit that most of these recipes are only medium-sweet. Please do adjust the sugar as you prefer. Similarly, as far as the nuts are concerned, you can add more or less as you like.

159

PHIRNI

Creamy Rice Pudding.
Also a rice and milk
combination like the previous
one, but quite different in
consistency—this one is smooth
and a little quicker to make.

INGREDIENTS
4 cups milk
3 ¹/₂ tablespoons ground rice (see note)
5-6 tablespoons sugar or to taste
Rose essence (optional)
15-20 almonds, blanched and thinly sliced

UTENSILS
A heavy bottomed pan
Serving dish or dishes

Method
1. Put the milk on to the fire in the pan. Let it come to a boil. Reduce heat.
2. Take a few tablespoons of hot milk and mix it with the ground rice to a smooth consistency. Mix into the milk on the fire.
3. Stir almost constantly. Cook till the milk is thickened and smooth. This will take about 10-15 minutes after you add the rice.
4. Add the sugar. Taste for sweetness. Simmer a few minutes, then take off the fire.
5. Add the essence and stir in the almonds, reserving a few for the garnish if you like.
6. Traditionally, this dish is served in individual little dishes with wide mouths. Pour it into them if you have them or put into a pretty serving bowl and refrigerate till needed.

Serves 4-6.

Note: To grind the rice, pick, wash and soak it in a little water for 15 minutes then drain out the water, reserving just as much as you need to grind it to a smooth puree. To dry grind it, wash earlier, dry throughly and then grind it. You can do this in a larger quantity and store for repeated use.

KHEER

Milk Pudding with Rice.
Creamy, rich and simmered
to perfection, this dessert is
special.

INGREDIENTS
8 cups milk
4 tablespoons rice, picked, washed and soaked
6-8 green cardamoms, roughly pounded
*   (discard the skins)*
*   20-30 almonds, blanched and*
*   sliced*
*   A handful of raisins*
*   5-6 tablespoons sugar*
*   or to taste*

*   UTENSILS*
*   A heavy bottomed*
*   pan or wok* (karhai)
*   A flat spoon*

Method

1. Into a pan, put the rice and milk. Discard the water in which the rice was soaked. Set the pan on the fire. On a medium fire, bring the milk to a simmering point. You have to keep stirring almost continuously to avoid the rice sticking to the bottom and burning. Once the milk is simmering, you can reduce the heat still further. You still have to stir frequently. You will notice that a thickish skin will keep forming on the top. Stir it back into the milk and continue cooking. The rice will get cooked in about 15 minutes. At this stage, add the cardamom, half the almonds and raisins. Stir and watch the pudding—you can take it off the fire when it has reduced to the consistency you desire. You should be able to see the grains of rice in it so it is not a totally smooth but slightly knobbly mixture. Add the sugar and stir to dissolve it. Taste to check sweetness.

2. Serve garnished with the remaining almonds. This dessert can be served hot or chilled.

Serves 4-6.

RABRI

Thickened, sweetened milk, made even richer by the addition of dry-fruit. A special dessert, indeed.

INGREDIENTS
8 cups milk
3-4 tablespoons sugar or to taste
A handful of almonds, blanched and sliced
Vark *(beaten silver) (optional)*

UTENSILS
A heavy-bottomed pan

Method

1. Set the milk on the fire. Bring to a boil, then reduce heat and simmer. Keep stirring, otherwise the milk may start sticking to the bottom and burning. Continue cooking till the milk is reduced to a thick, slightly lumpy consistency. It should take about 45 minutes.

2. Take off the fire, add the sugar and stir to dissolve it. Check sweetness.

3. Pour into a serving dish and garnish with the *vark* and almonds.

Makes 4 small servings.

RASGULLAS

Cottage cheese balls soaked in sugar syrup isn't really an apt description for this popular dessert. You have to try these spongy, soft rasgullas to believe how irresistible they are.

IN-s saffron

UTENSILS
A flat, heavy bottomed pan with a tight-fitting lid.
Another pan to curdle the milk
A muslin cloth

Method
1. Bring the milk to boiling point. Add a little vinegar. Keep adding it in little doses till the milk curdles completely i.e., a pale greenish liquid separates from the cheese. Strain the cheese and wash it well in a number of changes of water to ensure that there are no traces of vinegar left. Hang it up in a muslin cloth for about 40 minutes to allow the remaining water to drip away.
2. Put the drained cheese on a plate or in a food processor. Knead or blend to a smooth consistency.
3. Heat the water. Add the sugar to it. Let it dissolve completely. Skim away any impurities. Bring it to simmering point. Drop in the cardamom or saffron. Boil for a few minutes.
4. While the water-sugar mixture is heating up,   shape

the *rasgullas*. Each one should be about the size of a walnut. Drop them into the simmering syrup, cover the pan and let them remain on medium heat for 17-20 minutes. By this time the *rasgullas* will be puffed and spongy.
5. Carefully, remove the *rasgullas* into a serving bowl. Pour the sugar syrup over and refrigerate till needed.

Makes 10-11.

Note: In case you find the rasgullas *breaking (it is always useful to test one), you may knead 1-2 teaspoons flour into the dough. This can happen because of the fat content of the milk.*

165

RASMALAI

*Cottage Cheese Balls in
Thickened Milk.
Two delectable desserts in
one is what this recipe is all
about.*

INGREDIENTS
16 rasgullas
4 cups milk
Sugar to taste
*3-4 green cardamoms, peeled and ground
coarsely*
A few strands saffron

UTENSILS
A heavy bottomed pan

Method

1. Make *rasgullas* as in the last recipe except,
make them smaller. Before adding them to the
milk, drain them from the syrup for at least
an hour.

2. Put the milk on the fire. Bring to a boil, then
reduce heat and stirring frequently, cook till
slightly reduced and thickened. Stir in the sugar
and cardamom. Simmer a few minutes then take
off the fire. Drop in the saffron. Cool.

3. Pour into a serving dish and float the rasgullas
in the thickened milk.

4. Refrigerate till needed.

Serves 4.

*Note: Personally, I do not thicken the milk to
the consistency of* rabri. *I like to keep it
quite thin and runny. You may make it as
you prefer.*

KULFI

*Ice cream with Almonds.
Can you think of anything
better than a well-chilled
kulfi after a spicy, rich
meal?*

INGREDIENTS
*6 cups milk
3-4 tablespoons sugar or to taste
50-60 almonds, blanched and slivered
16 green cardamoms, peeled and powdered
A few drops of almond essence (optional)*

UTENSILS
*A heavy-bottomed wok and a slotted spoon.
6-7 kulfi moulds or glace ice moulds.*

Method
1. Put the milk into the pan and bring it to
simmering point. Stirring almost continuously,
which is essential to prevent lumps forming and
also to prevent the milk
sticking and burning,
cook till the milk is
reduced by more than
half. Keep stirring
the skin that forms
occasionally back
into the milk.

2. Add the sugar. Stir to dissolve it. Taste for
sweetness. At this stage, it should be over-sweet.
3. Remove from the fire and add the almonds
and cardamoms.
4. Stir in the almond essence. Cool.
5. Pour into the moulds and freeze.
6. Keep out to soften for about 10 minutes
before serving, then press the *kulfi* out
of the moulds. The plastic moulds are easier
to handle.

Makes 6-9.

*Note: This is a kulfi very rich in nuts. You can
reduce the quantity if you prefer, as also try
pistachios instead of almonds or in addition to
them. The other essences which also taste
equally good are pista and kesar.
You may also like to cheat a little. To thicken
the milk faster, add 1-2 teaspoons cornflour to
it before adding the sugar.
The number of kulfis you will get depends on
the size of moulds you will use.*

HALWA

Wheat Dessert.
Apart from enjoying this wheat-based
dessert (and it goes particularly well with
channa-bhaturas*), serve this to a fussy*
eater—it is a complete meal, incorporating
as it does wheat, ghee, *and sugar.*

INGREDIENTS
$^3/_4$ *-1 cup* ghee
1 cup, less 2 tablespoons, wheatflour, sieved
2 tablespoons semolina, sieved
3 cups water
1 cup sugar
Nuts and raisins
(optional)

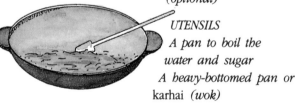

UTENSILS
A pan to boil the
water and sugar
A heavy-bottomed pan or
karhai *(wok)*

Method

1. Heat the *ghee.*
2. Add the flour and semolina. Stirring continuously, cook till the flour turns a golden brown and is aromatic.
3. While the flour is browning, boil the sugar and water. Stir to dissolve the sugar completely.

Take off the fire.
4. As soon as the flour browns, add the sugar-water. Keep stirring continuously. (You can wear oven gloves if you like as the water bubbles fiercely when it is added). As soon as you add the liquid, the flour will bind. Cook and stir continuously till the fat separates. Take off the fire and serve immediately, garnished with the nuts and raisins.

Serves 4-6.

Note: This traditional recipe is heavy. You
might like to put a little less fat and sugar or
alternately, remove some ghee *off the top after*
it is cooked. You may also like to experiment
with low-calorie oil instead of ghee.
To avoid last-minute activity, you can roast the
flour (without fat) earlier. Thereby you will
practically omit step 2.

GAJRELA

*Carrot Dessert.
Fresh winter carrots
simmered in milk make for
a delectable dessert. It
freezes excellently too.*

INGREDIENTS
1 kg milk
1 kg carrots, scraped and grated
Sugar to taste (approx. $^3/_4$-1 cup)
5-6 tablespoons oil or ghee
A few green cardamoms, peeled and crushed
*3-4 tablespoons nuts (almonds and pistachios),
blanched and slivered*
Raisins to taste (optional)

UTENSILS
A heavy-bottomed pan
A grater or food processor

Method
1. Warm the milk and add the carrots. Let the mixture simmer on low heat till all the milk has been absorbed. You have to keep stirring occasionally to prevent the mixture sticking at the bottom and burning.
2. Add the sugar and stir well to dissolve completely.
3. Add the oil or *ghee* and fry, stirring almost constantly till the mixture changes colour to a lightish brown and the fat separates.
4. Add the cardamoms and keep cooking another 5 minutes. You can add the raisins and nuts too at this time unless you prefer to garnish the *gajrela* with them, in which case, take it off the fire, turn into a serving dish and decorate with the nuts.

Serves 6.

Note: Gajrela *freezes excellently for months. You
can make it in large quantities when the
carrots are fresh and put it away for later
months.*

SHEER KHORMA

Rich Vermicelli Dessert.
Very rich, and very festive,
this is certainly a special
occasion dessert.

INGREDIENTS
1 cup ghee
1 cup almonds, blanched and sliced
¹/₂ cup raisins
1 cup magaz
³/₄ cup chironjee
¹/₂ cup cashew nuts, chopped
5-6 cloves
2 small pieces cinnamon
6-7 green cardamoms, pounded
250 gms vermicelli (sewiyan)
8 cups milk
1 cup dates, soaked in hot water and chopped fine
1 cup sugar or to taste
¹/₂ cup rose water

UTENSILS
A heavy-bottomed karhai (wok) or other large pan

Method
1. Heat the *ghee*. Don't allow it to start smoking.

2. Drop in the whole spices and dry fruit.
3. After a few minutes, drop in the vermicelli. Fry till very aromatic. The vermicelli will turn a goldenish colour.
4. Stirring continuously, add the milk and the dates. Let the whole mixture simmer till much of the milk gets absorbed.
5. Add the sugar. Stir to dissolve it. Take off the fire.
6. Sprinkle over the rose water. Serve immediately if you want to serve it hot otherwise cool and refrigerate till needed.

Serves 12-15.

Note: This recipe, being traditionally a festive one, made on Eid *days, is very rich in nuts,* ghee *and sugar. You can decrease the sugar and nuts if you like. As for the* ghee, *you do need a larger quantity to fry the vermicelli. However, you can skim off some from the top after the cooking process is over, if you like.*

MOOCHEIN

Sweet Vermicelli.
Inspite of its slightly strange, though not
wholly inexplicable name, Moochein—
meaning moustache — is another rich
dessert—vermicelli fried and immersed in a
sugar syrup.

INGREDIENTS
2 cups ghee
250 gms vermicelli, preferably the fine variety
2 cups sugar
1 cup water
5-6 green cardamoms
A few strands saffron
A few tablespoons rose water
Chopped, mixed nuts, to taste
1-2 tablespoons raisins

UTENSILS
Two large pans

Method

1. Heat the *ghee*. Don't let it start smoking.
2. Drop in the vermicelli. Fry golden brown.

Drain it from the *ghee*. You may put the *ghee* away for reuse. You will not be needing it any more for this recipe.
3. Put the sugar and water on to the fire. Stir to dissolve the sugar, then boil till the syrup is of one string consistency. Reduce heat. Drop in the cardamoms. Simmer five minutes more.
4. Add the saffron and rose water.
5. Immerse the fried vermicelli into the syrup. Stir to coat well. Simmer 5-8 minutes.
6. Take off the fire and stir in the nuts and raisins.
7. This can be served hot or at room temperature. It keeps for at least a week.

Serves 12.

SANDESH

*Sweet Cheese Fudge.
A section on Indian sweets
could hardly be complete
without this speciality from
Bengal*

INGREDIENTS

4 cups skimmed milk

A few tablespoons curds, whey or lemon juice
1½ -2 tablespoons sugar or to taste, ground
Ghee or oil
4 green cardamoms, peeled and ground
Pistachios, chopped

UTENSILS

A plate to knead on
A heavy bottomed pan
A strainer or muslin cloth
A baking tray with low sides

Method

1. Heat the milk. When it comes to boiling point, stir in some of the curds, lemon juice or whey. Reduce the heat and keep stirring and adding the curds till the milk curdles i.e., the cheese separates and a pale greenish liquid comes to the top. Take off the fire and drain, either through a muslin cloth or fine strainer. Keep the cheese aside to drain for at least 3-4 hours.

2. Put the drained cheese on a plate, sprinkle the sugar all over and knead the mixture. Do this alternately with your knuckles and palm of the hand till the mixture is absolutely smooth. Taste to check sweetness.

3. Put into a pan. On a slow fire, stirring almost continuously, cook till the mixture is dry. It should take about 10 minutes.

4. Grease the tray. Press down the mixture into it. Sprinkle the ground cardamoms and pistas all over. Mark lightly into squares and leave to cool. Remove the squares from the tray and store in an air-tight box. Preferably refrigerate.

Note: Instead of pressing down into a tray, you can press it into special moulds made for the purpose, in which case you can make it in pretty shapes.

KAJU BARFI

*Cashewnut Fudge.
An old family recipe that
has come down to me from
my late grandmother.*

INGREDIENTS
½ cup water
500 gms sugar
1 tablespoon milk
1 kg cashewnuts
A little water
3 teaspoons ghee or oil

UTENSILS
An electric or manual grinder
A heavy bottomed pan
A number of baking trays with low sides

Method

1. Put the water and sugar into the pan. On a slow fire, keep stirring to dissolve the sugar. Once the sugar is dissolved, you can raise the heat and let the mixture come to a boil.
2. Pour in the milk. It will attract impurities. Skim it off.

3. Strain the liquid through a fine muslin cloth or strainer.
4. Grind the cashewnuts with as much water as is needed to make a completely smooth paste.
5. Mix the ground paste with the sugar and oil or *ghee* and put back on the fire. Stir hard to mix it well. Cook on a slow fire till the mixture thickens and the fat separates.
6. Lightly grease the trays and press the *barfi* mixture onto it. Mark into diamonds or squares and let it cool.
7. Remove from the tray and store in an air-tight box.

Makes about 1½ kgs.

Note: In the refrigerator, this barfi *keeps well for many months.*

BESAN BARFI

Gramflour Fudge.
Heavy but truly delectable,
this barfi *is different from*
all the others because
instead of being milk-
based, it is made of
gramflour.

INGREDIENTS
750 grams ghee
1 kg gramflour, sifted
800 grams sugar, ground
5-6 cardamoms, peeled and powdered
(optional)
250 grams mixed nuts, chopped fine (optional)

UTENSILS
A heavy-bottomed pan
A large tray with low sides

Method
1. Heat the *ghee.*
2. Add the gramflour. Keep stirring almost continuously. Gradually, the flour will start to change colour and will become aromatic. It is best to stir in a circular motion, bringing the flour from the bottom to the top. Also keep scraping the bottom occasionally to ensure that the flour does not stick to the bottom and burn. Gradually the mixture will become considerably lighter in consistency. You will almost feel this happening as you stir. The flour will also by this time be a rich golden colour. Take off the fire.
3. Add the sugar and stir immediately and vigorously to blend it in well.
4. Add the nuts and cardamom. Stir to blend in.
5. Grease the tray lightly. Lay the mixture on to it evenly, smoothing the top.
6. Mark out squares and leave to cool. Remove from the tray and store in an air-tight box.

Makes about 2 ¹/₂ kgs.

Note: You may like to wear oven gloves while you're making this, as the mixture does bubble considerably.

178

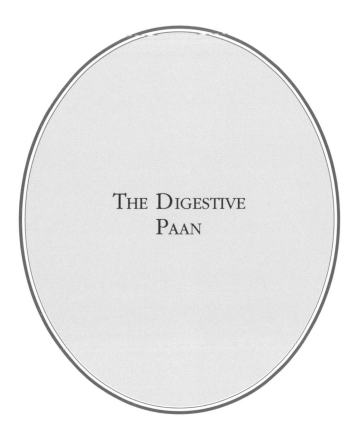

THE DIGESTIVE
PAAN

PAAN JOHRI

My father puts this paan *together at home. Most of the ingredients that go into it are homemade too.*

For the uninitiated, the paan *is a combination of a number of digestives—cardamom* (elaichi)*, aniseed* (sonf)*, supari, cloves* (laung)*—all neatly wrapped up in a betel leaf of your choice. If you buy it at a* paan *shop you can also decide whether or not you want it wrapped in* vark*, a thin sheet of beaten silver.*

This recipe has its own little history. It was given to my grandfather by a Mr. Johri who assured him that a paan *a day would keep many ills at bay, particularly for those suffering from stomatitis, blisters in the mouth etc—all signs of an unhealthy digestive system. One thing is for sure. It is what you need after a heavy Indian meal to help the food along its way. Even if you can't always get the betel leaves, keep at least the ground aniseed handy. The quantities for all the ingredients here will certainly serve you many times over. Store them in clean air-tight jars.*

INGREDIENTS
1 cup aniseed
1-2 tablespoons sugar
Green cardamoms
Churi *or* supari
Gulukand

Sugar
Any paan *masala*
Betel leaves

UTENSILS
A serving plate
A bowl to soak the paans
Decorative bowls for the ingredients
Small spoons

Method

1. Roast the aniseed lightly on a griddle till it changes a few shades darker.
Grind with the sugar to as coarse or as fine a consistency as you like. Check the sugar and add more if you like.
Store in an air-tight bottle.

2. The *churi* is a Rajasthani speciality. Aniseed is soaked in a betelnut solution and then dehydrated. If you cannot get it, use any *supari* you can get conveniently.

3. To make the *gulukand*, you need to collect about 500 gms of rose petals, preferably from red and pink roses of a non-grafted variety, which have a strong fragrance. In an airtight glass jar, alternately layer the rose petals with a thin sprinkling of sugar. Keep out in the sun for at least two weeks during which time the sugar will dissolve completely and the rose petals will turn blackish. Shake the jar occasionally during this time. Store the *gulukand* too in a clean, dry place.

4. The *paan masala*, is also a commercially sold preparation. Buy any brand you like, which doesn't contain tobacco.

To make the Paan

Wash the betel leaves well and soak in cold water for about 30 minutes. When you're ready to serve, shake each *paan* dry as you make it. On each, first smear a little *paan masala*. Add a teaspoon of the *churi* or *supari*, a teaspoon of ground aniseed, 1 green cardamom, and 1 teaspoon of *gulukand*. Fold into a triangle. To do this, lay the leaf with the broad side towards you on your left palm. With your other hand, fold the right side of the leaf over to the left edge. Similarly, fold the left side to meet the other edge, being careful not to spill any of the contents. Finally, fold the tip over towards yourself to make a neat triangle. Hold it together with a clove. This recipe makes a sweet *paan*. For those who prefer a *saada* one, i.e., one without sugar, omit the *gulukand*.

If you want to avoid last-minute activity, the *paans* can be made in advance and kept. Remember to keep the *saada* and *meetha* ones separately.

GLOSSARY OF PULSES, HERBS & SPICES

aniseed	:	*saunf*
asafoetida	:	*hing*
basil	:	*tulsi*
bayleaf	:	*tez patta*
bengal gram	:	*channa dal*
black gram	:	*urad dal*
black pepper	:	*kali mirch*
cardamom	:	*elaichi*
cinnamon	:	*dalchini*
cloves	:	*laung*
cumin	:	*zeera*
cumin (black)	:	*shahzeera*
coriander, cilantro	:	*dhania*
curry leaf	:	*kari patta*
fenugreek	:	*methi*
garlic	:	*lasun*
ginger	:	*adrak*
gramflour	:	*besan*
lentil	:	*masoor dal*
mace	:	*javitri*
mango powder	:	*amchoor*
mint	:	*pudina*
mustard	:	*rai or sarson*
nigella	:	*kalonji*
nutmeg	:	*jaiphal*
pomegranate seeds	:	*anardana*
poppy seeds	:	*khus khus*
red gram (split)	:	*arhar or tuar dal*
red kidney beans	:	*rajmah*
saffron	:	*kesar*
seasame seeds	:	*til*
split green gram	:	*dhuli moong dal*
tamarind	:	*imli*
turmeric	:	*haldi*
thymol seeds	:	*ajwain*
whole green gram	:	*sabut moong*
whole lentils	:	*sabut masoor*

GARAM MASALA

2 2" sticks cinnamon; 10 whole cloves;
1 heaped teaspoon whole, black peppercorns
Seeds of 5 black cardamoms; 5-6 green cardamoms
(use the skins too); 1 teaspoon grated nutmeg
(optional).

Grind all the above ingredients together as finely as
possible and store in an airtight jar. You may double
or treble the ingredients depending on your requirements but remember, there's nothing like freshly
ground *masala. Makes about 6 tablespoons.*

SAMBHAR POWDER

$1^1/_2$ tablespoons coriander seeds; 1 tablespoon
fenugreek seeds; 1 tablespoon red gram (split)
1 tablespoon bengal gram; 3/4 tablespoon turmeric
powder; 1-2 tablespoon chilli powder; 3/4 tablespoon
black pepper (ground).

Dry roast the coriander seeds, fenugreek seeds and
pulses together on a tava or any flat, heavy-bottomed
pan for a few minutes till they start to darken. You
have to keep stirring with a flat spatula to avoid any of
them burning. Grind and mix in the rest of the
ingredients and store in an airtight jar.
Makes about 6-8 tablespoons

VINDALOO POWDER

A small piece of cinnamon; 1 teaspoon cloves,
2 teaspoon cumin seeds; 8 teaspoons coriander
seeds; 2 teaspoons mustard seeds; $^1/_2$ teaspoon black
pepper; 6 red chillies or to taste; 2 teaspoons
turmeric powder.

Roast all the spices except for the turmeric in a   *karhai*
or on a griddle. You may also do it in an oven
preheated to 150°C. The spices should brown lightly
and become aromatic. Grind them. Add the turmeric
powder, mix well and store in an air-tight jar.
Makes about 6 tablespoons